LIVE A LIVE

The Complete Guide & Walkthrough with Tips &Tricks to Become a Pro Player

Walkthrough

Before we move on though, let's quickly cover some aspects of this guide worth noting before jumping in:

Everything optional that I recommend completing will be marked with an "optional" sub-heading in the guide. If you want to skip it, scroll down to the next heading that doesn't include the "optional" sub-heading to continue the main story.

At the end of every chapter with multiple party members, I'll note the "point of no return" moment. Why am I doing this? Well, aside from allowing you to go explore before the mission ends, this is your opportunity to equip all your best gear on your main protagonist or put it back in your inventory. We'll need these items for the Final Chapter and they need to be on the protagonist for that to happen.

The order of the missions below isn't a recommended order to play the chapters in. Play them in any order you feel like, although I'd recommend Prehistory, Imperial China or Near Future as good starting points. If you want more pointers about where to start, check out our Tips and Tricks section.

Live A Live Walkthrough

With that out of the way, feel free to select whichever chapter you're currently playing through via the list below:

Prehistory

Imperial China

Twilight of Edo Japan

The Wild West

Present Day

The Near Future

The Distant Future

The Middle Ages

The Final Chapter

Oersted's Final Chapter

Endings

Prehistory

Long before shinobis battled demon Lords and robots had to escape nightmarish creatures aboard spaceships, a young caveman is about to set off on a daring mission, battling mammoths and cultists to save the girl he loves. This tale is known as the Prehistory chapter and is one of Live A Live's longer sections.

That means there's a lot going on in Pogo's story, so for those looking for every optional boss, secret piece of equipment and crafting recipe, the walkthrough below has you covered.

Looking for a specific section of this chapter? Jump between sections using the links below:

Prehistory

Prehistory will begin with cutscenes depicting a cult of bandits, a kidnapped woman and a green-haired boy running from a group of particularly angry mammoths. Once it's all over, we'll get to name the aforementioned mammoth-hating green-haired boy. The default name for this character is Pogo (and we'll be referring to him as that throughout the chapter), but you can name him whatever you like.

Once that's done, confirm the name and we'll cut to Pogo sleeping in a cave. Once he wakes up, search the stone cupboards in the top left-hand corner. You'll find a Stick. With that in your inventory, head south through the cave's exit. As you leave, Pogo's best friend Gori (the gorilla we saw in the intro) will wake up too, joining the party.

As you leave, you'll run into a snoozing caveman. Talk to him to wake him up. He'll make some worried grunts before pointing to the path leading west. It seems that's the way we want to go. Before we head there, let's go through the door to the right of the one leading to Pogo's room. Inside, we'll find a caveman in the back left-hand corner and several cabinets on the right. Loot the cabinets to find a Stick, a Pelt and a Bone.

Optional: The Hay Stack Game

Now, talk to the caveman. He'll play a game with you and reward you with supplies if you win. The game is simple:

When talking to the caveman, his grunt bubbles will show two pictures containing either five cavemen, three cavemen or a gorilla. He'll then point to one of these two pictures:

If he points to five cavemen, he wants you to pick the haystack with the most cavemen in it.

If he points to three cavemen, he wants you to pick the haystack with the least cavemen in it.

If he points to the gorilla... well... no prizes for what he wants you to find (it's the gorilla).

You'll then see all the cavemen and a potential gorilla run into the haystacks. Make a choice and, if you're successful, you'll win a bunch of resources. Play as many times as you like (the resources are infinite) and then leave the cave.

Head west and through the door indicated to us by the sleeping caveman earlier. We'll enter a large hub area filled with cavemen.

Before we press on with the story, let's stop in and talk to the item crafter. From the centre of the hub area, head southwest. You'll find another tunnel with a tool emblem above it.

Optional: Crafting

Inside, you'll find a vendor. If you give this vendor certain items, he'll be able to combine them, giving you great gear from the offset.

There's a long list of equipment you can make here by merging and combining items, but let's get you kitted out with some of the best ones. If you need more crafting items, head back to the haystack mini-game. Every time you win, you'll get a bunch of materials.

Now, let's rustle up some good gear. Below I'll list recipes that make powerful gear. Everything listed below can be acquired from the Haystack Mini-Game:

Crafting Recipe	Created Item
Bone + Hard Rock	Stone Knife
Bone + Stone Knife	Quick Spear
Dried Skins + Stone Knife	Wildheart Armour
Bone + Pelt	Beastskin Cap
Dried Skins + Hard Rock	Bang Glove
Beast Horn + Bone	Rough Bands
Beast Fang + Dried Skins	Laughing Mask
Pelt + Stone Knife	Leather Strap
Hard Stone + Stone Knife	Fertility Charm
Leather Strap + Stone Knife	Fury Knife

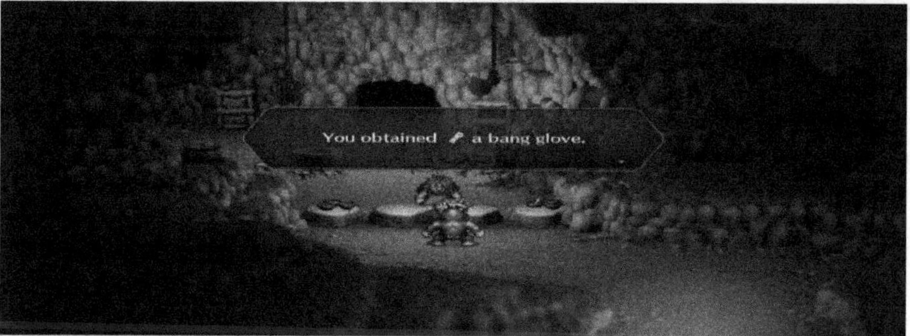

The items above contain a mix of armour, weapons and accessories. Craft and equip what you'd like, and then we'll proceed with the level.

The Elder's Request

Return to the hub area and look for a tunnel with a horseshoe emblem above it. It's on the left-hand side of the cave. Inside, you'll find the tribe elder. He'll grunt at Pogo and Gori, before exiting the area through the same door we entered through. Loot the cupboard to your left to find a Stick and then follow him.

Once back in the hub area, head through the central tunnel. Continue following the path and take a right, heading up and out of the cave. You'll find the elder chatting with a caveman nearby. Talk to the elder and we'll see a short demonstration, as the nearby caveman battles a plume of white smoke and emerges with a slab of meat. That's our cue. You're getting booted out of the nest... bring back some food or don't come back at all.

After you've recovered, you'll learn about scents. Hit the Y button to engage Pogo's smell-o-vision. It'll cause scent clouds to appear. Run into one and see what symbol comes up.

If it's a deer, that means food's nearby. Look for a small cloud of dust on the floor and walk up to it to initiate an encounter. Every time you win one of these encounters, you'll get a Haunch of Meat. We need three to return to the cave.

They shouldn't be too difficult to find. There's a scent just south of the elder, another slightly east of the first and a third south of the second, next to some dinosaur bones. You can also find a fourth scent to the far east of the area, but it isn't essential to the objective. The enemies you'll fight are dogs, boars and deer, so they won't pose much of a threat. Hit them with Pow Kick, Bang Bash or Bang Slap to vanquish them.

As we're fighting low-level enemies, this is a good time to learn Pogo and Gori's move sets, which are pretty basic compared to Live A Live's more civilised characters. Pogo has Pow Kick and Bang Bash (both deal low damage). Meanwhile, Gori has Bang Slap, which deals medium damage, and Scare Face, which deals low damage. Both characters will gain more abilities as the chapter goes on, but for now, the combat is mostly about smart positioning and melee.

When you've gathered all three slabs of meat, head back to the elder and turn them in. He'll allow you back into the cave. Once inside, head to Pogo and Gori's bedroom. It's the location we woke up in at the start of the chapter. Gori will go straight to sleep. Head to your bed and walk over it to go to sleep.

Finding Beru

When Pogo wakes up, Gori will have disappeared. We can track him via his scent. Turns out the gorilla has walked to the cave's storage room while asleep. Leave Pogo's room, head west and enter the hub area. Look for a tunnel on the right-hand side of the cave with a bone emblem over the entrance.

Inside, you'll find Gori asleep on the floor. Wake him up. Once he's awake, leave the room. You'll watch a short cutscene of someone grabbing a slab of meat from the nearby pile. After you emerge in the hub area, return to the food storage room.

Once inside, prod the hay pile you saw the hand emerge from (it's directly to the right of the meat pile). Someone will emerge from the pile, causing Pogo and Gori to flee. Return to the hay piles. We'll now have to prod each stack the thief is hiding in. This is the order:

prod the stack on the far right.

Prod the second haystack from the left.

Prod the second haystack from the right.

After the person moves, smell their scent (it'll conjure an image of a flower) and then prod the same haystack again.

The haystack will get up and move across the room, sitting in the corner. Walk back to the pile of food and grab the final Haunch of Meat, then head over to the haystack and offer the slab of food to the mysterious person. Leave the room and return once again. The meat will be gone. When you approach the haystack this time, the person will reveal themselves to be a woman called Beru; the same woman we saw escape the cult of bandits earlier.

After a short interaction, Beru will join Pogo's party. Wake up Gori and then leave the cave. Our goal now is to return to Pogo's room. When you get to the tunnel leading to the room, Pogo will realise the sleepy guard is in the doorway again. He'll ditch Gori and Beru, attempting to move the guard. Walk up to him and interact to try to push him out of the way. The plan won't work.

After you regain control, head back to the meat room and interact with the hay pile we found Beru in. Pogo will grunt about her using the haystack as a disguise, at which point she'll throw it over her head. Now, return to Pogo's room. This time you'll be able to freely move the guard. Once inside the room, head over to Pogo's bed and get in.

Pogo will realise that Beru doesn't know where to sleep, getting up and violently kicking Gori out of bed. Eventually, Beru will lie in the bed and go to sleep.

Hiding Beru

The next morning, Pogo will wake up to find Gori in his bed instead of Beru. After you regain control, head to the haystack in the corner. Examine it and you'll find Beru asleep beneath. Just as she's about to chat to Pogo (or, uh, softly grunt at him, I guess?), Gori will get punched through the doorway by a member of the tribe.

The tribesman will accuse the pair of stealing the meat Beru ate. Eventually, he'll leave. After he's gone, Pogo will hear Beru's stomach growling and land a new objective: find food. Return to the field where the elder sent us to scrounge food last time, exiting via the central tunnel in the hub area.

Talk to the caveman guarding the cave to access the hunting fields. Sniff for animals, track one down and win the encounter to get another Haunch of Meat. Take the meat all the way back to Beru in Pogo's room.

Once you've given her the food, she'll kiss Pogo. After you've got that reaction, head to the main hub of the cave.

This is the last time we'll be in here, so let's use it wisely. If you want to craft items, now's the time. Play the haystack mini-game, hunt in the wilderness and do anything else you feel is crucial before we depart.

When you're ready, use the central tunnel that leads to the exit. However, don't make a right this time. Instead, talk to the caveman blocking the north doorway.

After Pogo gets sucker punched by the guard, the bandits we saw at the beginning of the chapter will drive through the doorway in stone carts. When Pogo regains consciousness, head towards the cave's hub area.

As we're about to reach the hub, we'll watch a cutscene where the cult's mysterious red-haired leader interrogates the tribe elder. He asks where Beru is, but the elder doesn't know. The bandits eventually find Beru, bringing her to the bandit's leader. When we regain control, head into cave's hub area.

After a short interaction where Pogo frees Beru by accidentally falling in the bandits' stone cart, we'll have to fight five of the bandits. The numbers may seem intimidating, but this is a simple fight. The bandits don't hit particularly hard, while Pogo, Beru and Gori all have attacks that will one-shot their opponents. Focus on Bang Bash (Pogo), Bang Slap (Gori) and Bam Bam Bam (Beru).

Following the fight, we'll take on the bandits' leader: Zaki. Zaki has a ranged attack where he throws lizards at opponents directly above, below, left, right or diagonal to him. This is fairly weak, however, his melee hit can be pretty punishing. Using Pow Hit, Zaki can land a decent amount of damage on the team if he gets in close, making it more beneficial to rely on ranged moves.

If Pogo and Gori both levelled up in the last fight, they should have Stench Poot and Poop Throw (the two classiest ways to defeat an opponent), making it easier to have an all-out ranged fight.

When he's down, we'll cut to a scene where he retreats with his men. Pogo will then plead with the elder to let Beru stay with the tribe, but this cold Gandalf knock-off is having none of it. He banishes Pogo, Gori and Beru, leaving them at the mercy of the wilderness.

Banished

When we regain control, we'll be out in the wild. We have to head north from here, through the wilderness, although there's a catch. Random encounters are scattered across our path. We can sniff them out using Pogo's scent powers, although it's inevitable that we're going to end up in a few scraps.

Although the random encounters can be frustrating, they're a great way to boost the power of all three of your party members, which is hugely important considering we have some intimidating opponents ahead. Don't be scared to grind here. Reaching a level between 8 - 10 for your party members will do a lot in the long run, especially as Beru will leave the gang soon and not return until the final boss fight. It might be worth sticking on some tunes and defeating some mammoths for half an hour.

If you are going to grind here, there are a couple of things to note. For one, there are bound to be a few enemy encounters that are too hard to take on when you first enter the wilderness. If you run into battles where the odds are stacked against you, simply flee and come back later. Secondly, there's another item crafter in the northwest section of this area, so head to him if you want to craft some equipment.

When you are ready to move on, let's head to the cave northeast of where we arrived in the area. It's marked by the golden diamond on your map. Once inside, a cutscene will play, with Pogo, Gori and Beru sitting around a fire. After a moment where Gori gets beaten up for causing an explosion with his farts (no, I'm not making that up), the trio will go to sleep.

Zaki Rematch

In the middle of the night, Beru will get kidnapped, with the bandits whisking her away. When you regain control, head through the exit northwest of the fire. As

Pogo attempts to follow the group, he's stopped by Zaki, who demands a rematch. A battle will ensue. This is pretty similar to the first Zaki showdown, although it'll just be Pogo taking him on.

Considering Zaki has no vulnerabilities, the best bet is to rely on your stronger attacks. If you got Pogo to at least level 8 then we should have some attacks that fit the bill.

Burn Spark will hit for huge damage, meanwhile, Whee Jump will let you land big shots from afar (which is useful for dodging his melee move). Finally, Yum Bite will allow you to heal and Poke Bind will potentially bind him, so both are useful manoeuvres.

Zaki's move set won't have changed much, although he will have a more powerful variant of his lizard-throwing ranged move. Hit him hard and he'll go down in no time.

Once the fight's done, Zaki will flee further into the cave, sealing the path behind him. Go wake Gori when you regain control (he's by the entrance to the cave). Once he's up, walk him to the now-sealed exit and interact with it. Gori will break through, allowing us to access the next portion of the cave.

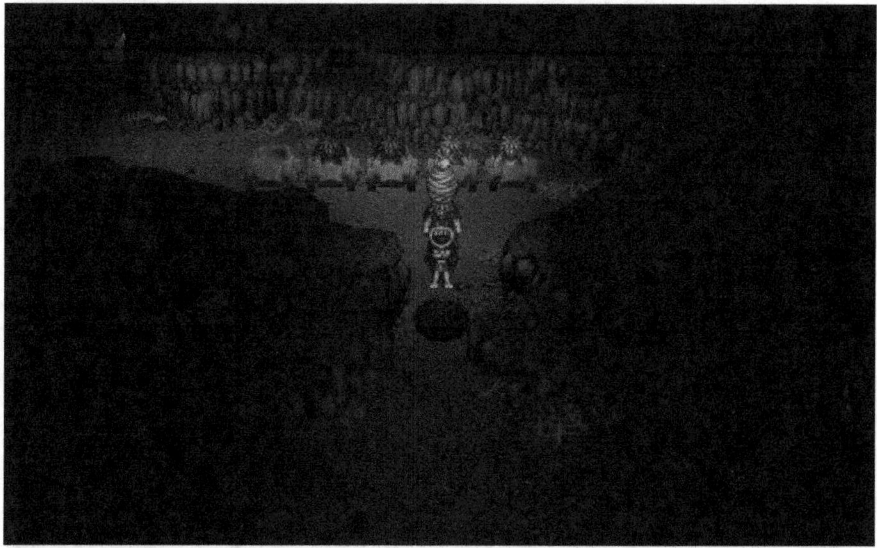

We'll run into Zaki and Beru again. However, just as it looks like the pair might save Beru, Zaki will send Pogo and Gori plummeting down a hidden hole.

Cave Depths

After the pair have fallen, Pogo will awaken in the field of flowers he dreamt he was in with Beru. We'll regain control here. Run north. After a while, Pogo will come across Beru picking flowers with her back turned to him.

As he approaches her, she turns, revealing it's just Gori in a pink wig. Pogo will then wake up to realise he's just in the cave's depths with Gori slumped on top of him. Time to escape this hell hole.

Head around to the back of the cave, using the route east of where you woke up. Once you reach the path around the back of this area, use Pogo's scent power. Run into the scent bubbles until you find a picture of Zaki. It should be just north of the mound you awoke on. Once you find it, move to the cave wall just north of the scent bubble and interact with it when prompted. Pogo will slam into it but it won't give way. Continue to interact with it until it does give way, bringing us back to the area with the fire pit.

Optional: King Mammoth Secret Boss

Before we press on, there's an optional secret boss in this section that we can choose to defeat if we want. However, I'll put it bluntly. This is easily one of the hardest bosses in the entire game and it's a huge time investment, so don't worry about him if you aren't bothered about missing a few items. Not only does King Mammoth hit like a truck and have the ability to dodge 80% of your attacks, but he heals himself before you can inflict any real, lasting damage. That means we have to finish him before he can respond.

If you're game for the challenge, then head back into the wilderness area we crossed after first being banished. Roaming this area is a golden, fire-breathing mammoth known as King Mammoth, and he's particularly tedious to track down. He'll run around this stretch of wilderness in a seemingly random pattern, and to face him, we'll have to click "A" when his invisible avatar passes us by. However, before we track him, we have a long, long, LONG stint of grinding to do.

To face King Mammoth and be able to withstand his ridiculous stats, you'll need to be somewhere between level 16 and level 20. To do that, we just have to run through a ton of random encounters out in the wilderness. You'll just need to keep battling until you reach level 16 and unlock the Bing Bang Boom ability. This is the hail mary we need to secure our victory.

Once you're level 16 or higher, it's time to track King Mammoth. Use Pogo's smell-o-vision and walk through the smell bubbles until you see one featuring the picture of a mammoth. That means we're on to the King's scent. Look around and, if you're close to the giant elephant, you'll hear stomping and the screen will shake. Walk towards the sound of the stomping while repeatedly tapping A. If you cross paths with the King, a battle will initiate.

It can be hard to find King Mammoth at times due to how specific his positioning needs to be for the button push to register. Just keep trying and you should eventually manage to catch him. A good trick is to close in on him when he's trapped in a corner or up the ramp near the entrance to the northern cave. Save the game here and whenever you reload, you'll be able to catch him quickly. Now for the battle.

Right, the key to bringing down King Mammoth is all based on whether you get lucky in your strategy. Considering the King is so quick, most of your attacks won't land, and those that do will rarely leave any status effect. The main thing we want to do is firmly jam King Mammoth in the top left corner (as shown above). I'll explain why soon, but get in close and make sure you're standing in front of him rather than behind him.

If you're stood behind, he'll frequently use his fire AOE (known as Great Fire Boom). The attack hits hard and leaves fire tiles on the floor that hurt you and dramatically heal him. King Mammoth LOVES this move, so let's not give him any more reason to use it. He can still use the move if you're in front of him, but he's far more likely to rely on his melee trunk attack.

As the battle begins, get both party members up in his face and spam Poke Bind. We're trying to hit King Mammoth with the Paralysis status effect, which is based entirely on blind luck. While we're doing this, Gori will be used as support, drawing aggro from King Mammoth, placing poison tiles down with Poop Throw in place of fire ones and using Huge Haunches of Meat to keep you in the fight. If he doesn't need to heal you and there are no fire tiles in play, pass his turn. Pogo is the one with the power here.

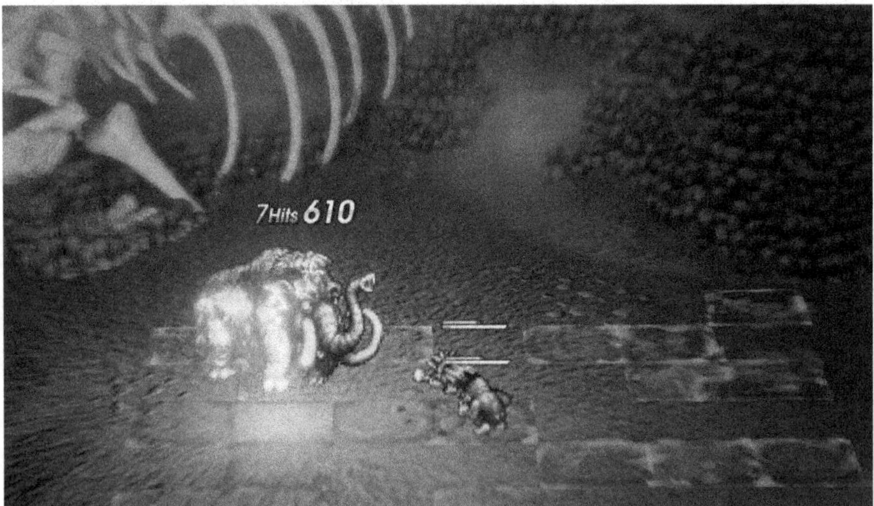

If the Poke Bind works and King Mammoth becomes paralysed, you need to capitalise on the opportunity immediately. Bust out Pogo's Bing Bang Boom attack (this is the move we unlocked at level 16). As the move can't miss anymore, it'll do huge damage to King Mammoth, likely knocking 700 hit points off his health bar. It can be tempting to immediately try and hit the move again, but now we have to play tactically. This is the true start of the battle.

With Mammoth's health dropped below half, he'll begin his second phase, adding his most powerful move to his arsenal: Mount Big Boom. He'll charge this but there's no point trying to evade or interrupt it. It's coming and the best thing you can do is prepare.

Once it's unleashed, the entire arena will be covered in fire tiles. Around one turn after this lands, King Mammoth will regenerate 200 health from the fire tiles, and then consistently regenerate around 70 health every few turns after that. We want to prevent his healing capabilities as much as possible.

This is why we needed to shove King into the corner. After the attack, as soon as its Gori's turn, execute Poop Throw and aim the projectile directly beneath the centre of King Mammoth. It'll turn all the fire tiles beneath him into poison tiles. That'll prevent him from healing and deal a tiny bit of damage. Now, we return to the original strategy. Pogo hits Poke Bind repeatedly until we get a paralysis status ailment.

This can take a long time, so keep turning the fire tiles to poison, healing and hitting Poke Bind. When the paralysis finally sets in, hit another Bing Bang Boom. If you're lucky, that should finish him off for good. As a reward for toppling this behemoth, you'll a Fang of the King and potentially a Cola Can... fitting rewards for slaying a beast with Wolverine-esque healing, speed matching Goku and the strength of Chris Redfield moving boulders.

All jokes aside, the Cola Can is actually a very useful item and a rare drop from King Mammoth. It will be a useful item in our fight during the Final Chapter. If it didn't drop for you in the fight and you want it, load a save and attempt to defeat King Mammoth again.

Picking Up Beru's Trail

With King Mammoth slain (or avoided), let's press on. When in the cave where Beru was kidnapped, head through the door we last saw Zaki exit through. It's just left of the campfire Gori blew up when he farted earlier in the chapter.

After entering, push forward, leaping over the hole in the floor. Now follow the path ahead until you exit through the opposite side of the cave. You'll emerge outside. Continue following the path until you see a small outcrop to the left. Head onto it and tap A until you find a Haunch of Meat. Return to the path and continue on.

You're inevitably going to run into some wildlife here, but it's nothing you haven't handled before. Push through, using your scent vision to avoid battles if you're not bothered about fighting. Once you reach the end of the path, you'll find a caveman south of you and a door north. If you want to craft any items, go talk to the caveman. Otherwise, let's continue inside.

You'll enter Kuu Village. There's a sleeping bandit guarding the door on the left, so head up the path on the right. Proceed to the edge of the outcrop ahead and you'll see some bandits walking two female gorillas between a pair of caves. This will make Gori angry. Once you regain control, leave Gori and walk back towards the entrance to Kuu Village.

As you're going down the path, Gori will burst past the sleeping bandit we saw earlier, leaving the party (and destruction in his wake). Head down the left path where the bandit used to be. We'll see three tunnels here.
The left and middle tunnels are bait-outs. All that's inside are battles against massive groups of angry bandits. If you're interested in using them to grind up some levels, head inside and use Big Shout to end the fight quickly. After you defeat the group, you'll be chased by two bandits, who will endlessly respawn.

When you're ready to move on, take the tunnel on the right. Inside, loot the stone cabinets ahead of you and on the left. You'll find some crafting materials.

As for what's in the centre of the tunnel, you'll find Gori, who's enjoying the attention of the female gorillas he saved earlier. Talk to him three times and Pogo will beat up Gori (the dude really can't catch a break), forcing him to rejoin the party.

Once you're reunited, head east and through the door at the end of the tunnel. We'll discover another fork in the road, with a door ahead of us and another to the right. Enter the room ahead and loot the cabinets at the back of the room. You'll find a Stick and a Bone. Now, return to the fork in the road and enter the door on the right.

You'll find yourself in a long tunnel with two cavemen. Kill them both and then proceed to the end of the tunnel. You'll see a door with a skull emblem above it. Enter to trigger a cutscene where a group of bandits attack Gori and Pogo before being beaten up by the gorillas Gori saved earlier.

Now, this is a big turning point. We can return to the main stretch of wilderness to find a rare secret or press on through the door ahead and take on the two final bosses. This final secret is worth the trek, but it's up to you.

Optional: Obtaining the Rock of Rocks

Assuming you're up for finding the final secret, we'll have to make our way back to the wilderness we were banished to earlier. That means returning all the way back to the cave Beru was kidnapped from and heading through the south exit.

Once you exit the cave, head to the edge of the small outcrop just to the left of the mouth of the cave (as pictured above). It can tricky to spot, but there's something new here.

A small stone resembling a human face will be overlooking the edge of the rocks. We'll be able to interact with this stone. This sounds ludicrous, I know, but interact with it 100 times.

Initially, it won't seem like you're doing anything, but it's definitely working. Once you hit 100, you'll hear a click.

Don't press it again. Instead, head to the northwest section of the area we're currently in. A sealed cave has opened. If you're struggling to find it, it's southwest of the wilderness item crafter.

Before we enter the cave. It's crucial you have a Bone in your inventory. If you do, enter the cave. Inside, you'll find a slab of stone eerily similar to 2001: A Space Odyssey's iconic monolith.

Approach it and give it a Bone. In return, it'll give you the Rock of Rocks. This seemingly useless item is actually incredibly useful, boosting your Special Attack rating significantly. With it acquired, let's return to the mission at hand.

Point of No Return Warning

This next section will wrap the chapter up, so let's make sure all our best equipment is stacked onto Pogo or in our inventory. Why should we do this?

Well, the game's Final Chapter will allow Pogo to bring all his gear and inventory with him to battle a new evil. However, he can't bring gear equipped to his fellow party members. Stack him with gear and then let's go.

Saving Beru

If you went to get the Rock of Rocks, return all the way back to the door in Kuu Village with the skull emblem over it. If you opted to skip the Rock of Rocks, you should already be there, so just head through. You'll enter another room with a large door. Enter it and a cutscene will play.

The cutscene will show the bandits praying to Beru, who's tied up on a sacrificial altar. Once you regain control, run towards the ritual. As you get close, Pogo will go Saitama-mode and take out several bandits with a few strikes. This will scare the remainder off. He'll then square off with Zaki, initiating a one-on-one fight between the two.

This is your third fight with Zaki and, by now, you're likely a lot stronger than him. He'll use his ranged lizard throw and a melee attack, but neither will do huge damage. To whittle his health away fast, just use strikes that inflict medium or high damage. If you're a high enough level, you'll have Fly Huge Boom, Burn

Sparks, Big Shout and maybe even Bing Bang Boom. All of these melt away his health bar.

Position yourself smartly and heal if need be. Before long, Zaki's health will falter. Just as he's about to fall, you'll hear a rumbling sound and the fight will end. The following cutscene will show the platform you fought Zaki on crumble beneath your feet, as Pogo, Gori, Beru, Zaki and the ritual leader all fall into the pit below. They'll awaken to see what made the rumbling noises.

The ritual leader will quickly be eaten, leaving the four survivors to face off against Ode; a giant, demonic dinosaur.

Odo Fight

As the fight begins, Zaki will join the party, helping Pogo, Gori and Beru topple their fearsome foe. This fight shouldn't be too bad depending on how high-level Pogo and Gori are. If you took down King Mammoth, you're likely so powerful that Odo will seem like child's play.

However, he still has a few solid attacks to watch out for. Up close, he has two melee attacks that inflict medium damage. Meanwhile, he has a diagonal power attack known as Swoop, that can hit hard if you aren't prepared.

Fortunately, there's no need for tactics or strategy when it comes to fighting back. Odo has no resistances or weaknesses, so just pummel him with any strong attacks you have. If Pogo has Fly Huge Boom or Whee Jump, use them. These are good damage dealers that will put Odo down quickly. Burn Spark and Bing Bang Boom will also eviscerate him if you have them.

Generally, anything that deals medium damage or above is enough to get the job done. Hit him with everything you have, heal when necessary and Odo will go down in no time. With the big dinosaur down for the count, the chapter is complete. Time to pick a new character.

Imperial China

With training montages, epic duels and mystical powers aided through the mastery of martial arts, the Imperial China chapter is one of Live A Live's most enthralling sections. Although it's largely story-based, there is a good amount of action to be found here as well.

If you're looking for a breakdown of where to go or how to defeat some of Shifu's stronger opponents, the walkthrough below will give you all the tips and tricks to conquer this section.

Looking for a specific section of this chapter? Skip between sections using the links below:

Imperial China	Beginning Our Journey	Yunfa Market	Bamboo Forest
Wong Village	Returning to the Peak of Mount Aspiration	Training	Dealing With The Bandits
The Attack on Aspiration Mountain	Indomitable Fist Fortress	The Revelry of Blood	Final Boss Battle

Imperial China

The chapter opens on a busy street, as the narrator spins the yarn of an elderly man tirelessly searching for a successor to prolong his ancient martial art. We'll then get to name this powerful fighting style. The default name is Earthen Heart, and so that's what we'll be calling it for the remainder of this chapter, but the name is really up to you.

We'll then meet the Shifu of Earthen Heart; a powerful master that's spent years in the mountains honing his abilities. He'll attempt to break a rock. When he fails, he'll come to the realisation that he's growing old and needs a successor, beginning a long journey to find his replacement.

Beginning Our Journey

In the next scene, we'll take control of Shifu in his mountainside Cottage. Head to the top left-hand corner of the cottage and grab the Qilin Boots and Weathered Boots from the two chests. Equip the Qilin Boots in your inventory, as they'll boost your defence and speed stats. Now, exit the cottage through the door at the bottom of the screen.

You'll emerge on the cliffs of Mount Aspiration. Loot the two White Clovers from the plants to the left of the house and then head west. You'll come across a diverging path, with steps leading up and down the mountain. Take the ones leading down. The ones leading up just lead to the peak of Mount Aspiration, where we saw Shifu punch the rock earlier. There's nothing to find up there right now.

Descend the first flight of steps and then head left, looking for a bush you can interact with. Shifu will find a Tuft of Birdeye Speedwell. After you've grabbed it, push east, continuing to descend the mountain. You'll eventually transition screens. Follow the path down until you reach a point where you can either go left or right.

From here, we'll have to access three different locations: the Bamboo Forest, Wong Village and Yunfa Market. We'll need to go to all of them to find worthy successors, although the order isn't preset, so go wherever the wind takes you. We'll run through each of the scenarios offered to you in each locale below:

Yunfa Market: Hong	Bamboo Forest: Lei	Wong Village: Yun

Yunfa Market: Hong

Yunfa Market can be found by heading east at the bottom of Mount Aspiration. The trail is marked by several carts and stalls, so you'll know you're going the right way.

When you arrive, you'll find yourself on a long high street. Talk to the locals if you like; they all know Shifu and are glad to see he's descended the mountain.

Keep pushing up the street and you'll run into a short cutscene, with a thief running from a shop eating a bowl of noodles while an angry shopkeeper attempts to slash him with a knife.

It's clear he's pretty nimble, managing to dodge the shopkeeper's blows with ease while continuing to eat. He'll eventually be caught by the townspeople, with the shopkeeper demanding he pays for his food. Once the scene's done, talk to the thief.

The shopkeeper will explain the thief steals his food regularly. He'll then tell Shifu to punish the thief. You can protest, but with no money to foot the bill, you have to fight him. A fight will ensue, with Shifu taking on the thief.

When in battle mode, approach the boy and hit him with Wise Fox's Grace. This will likely bind the thief and prevent him from attacking. Now, hit him with any of Shifu's moves. Generally, Shifu has a lot of fast-paced attacks that deal low damage but offer plenty of tactical advantage. He can retreat and attack in one move, create distance by shoving opponents and lower stats with ease, so get used to his playstyle when fighting weaker opponents like this thief.

It shouldn't take long to bring the thief down. After the fight's done, the shopkeeper will leave and Shifu will talk to the thief. The thief will tell him he steals because he's unable to get a job and hasn't the money to eat the food required to maintain his size and strength. Shifu will tell him he should see his size as a gift, and offer to train the boy in exchange for free meals. The thief will accept, revealing his name is Hong Hakka. That's our first disciple recruited.

Once he's in the pack, push to the top of town and find an old woman beneath a tarp (it's next to a broken pot of apples and a cart). She'll give you a Pork Bun.

After you've talked to her, continue up the street and find an old man next to a pile of green apples. He'll give you a Porcelain Bowl. Equip it on Shifu if he currently doesn't have a weapon. Now, head south and back to the bottom of the steps leading to Mount Aspiration.

Bamboo Forest: Lei

It's time to head to Bamboo Forest. From the base of Mount Aspiration, head west and follow the path straight, not descending the steps we'll see on the way. You'll eventually arrive at the entrance to a sprawling forest. Enter the area.

There are tigers roaming this area. They'll run for you and initiate a battle if they see you. You can pretty easily defeat them if you like, although Shifu doesn't gain experience, so it isn't essential. Run past them or take them down depending on your preference.

After your first tiger run-in, you'll enter a large clearing. Head to the top of the clearing and look for some grass on the right-hand side. Examine it and Shifu will find a Tuft of Nature's Providence. You can also find a Tuft of White Clover just above the clearing's exit. Grab that and then continue heading west.

Once you leave the clearing, follow the path up until you're encountered by a bandit, who will attempt to rob Shifu. When she asks for money, refuse to give it to her. This will initiate a battle. On the battlefield, approach the bandit and use Wise Fox's Grace to bind her, preventing her from getting off an attack. Now, use a combination of any of Shifu's attacks. It's best to use these disciple battles to get used to Shifu's move set, so experiment and see what works for you. The bandit will go down easily.

Once the battle is over, the bandit will lament being beaten by a man four times her age. Shifu will offer to train her in the art of kung-fu and she'll accept, claiming she wishes to know how he managed to defeat her. After the conversation, Lei Kugo will join you as a disciple.

Once the battle's done, we'll be in a small area with three diverging paths. Head down the one to the left. You'll arrive at a small outcrop with a tiger defending two patches of grass. Defeat the tiger and grab them both to find a Tuft of Birdeye Speedwell and a Tuft of Nature's Providence.

Return to the fork in the road, this time heading right. You'll find two tufts of grass. Loot the one on the left to find a Tuft of Nature's Providence. Return to the fork in the road again and head up the central path. You'll find a tiger guarding two tufts of grass. Defeat or evade it and loot the grass to find a Tuft of Nature's Providence and a Tuft of Shepherd's Purse.

There's a path leading to a palace if we continue pushing north, but we can't enter yet. Note its position though, as we'll have to return here at the end of the chapter. Once you've grabbed all the tufts of grass, leave the Bamboo Forest through where we entered. Return to the base of Mount Aspiration.

Wong Village: Yuan

Once you're back at the base of the steps leading to Mount Aspiration, head west and look for a set of steps leading down. They'll be near the beginning of the path leading to the Bamboo Forest. Descend the steps and head south. You'll eventually wind up in Wong Village.

Continue south through the town and look for an old woman on your left. She'll groan when you talk to her. The inventory will then open. Give her a Tuft of Nature's Providence (we should've found some in the Bamboo Forest if we visited the location before coming here). She'll be cured. She'll then reveal some information about her grandson, who may be a good recruit.

There are a few other elderly citizens suffering from the illness here. You'll find a patient north of the old woman, an old man southeast of her and an elderly lady south of her. All three of them will offer you items if you cure them, including an Iron Wok chest plate, a Catfish Whisker helmet and a Pork Bun.

You'll find a final patient northeast of the shirtless guard at the bottom of Wong Village, however, the Nature's Providence won't heal her. Turns out, she's just really, really hungry (I've been there buddy). You can give her a Pork Bun if you like, but she won't offer any reward, so there's not much point.

When you're ready, talk to the shirtless guard at the bottom of town. We'll watch a short scene where the old woman's grandson is being hassled by a gang. Turns out he's been forced to steal from Shifu for the gang, but is refusing to be a part of their scheme any longer.

Once the scene's done, talk to the shirtless guard again. He'll tell Shifu to walk away. Select "Pardon Me" and Shifu will teleport passed the guard, walking towards the gang. After a short conversation, Shifu will initiate a fight with the three men.

To beat the criminals, hit each of them with Monkey's Withdrawal. As they're weak to the move, the two lackeys will go down in one hit, while the leader will take two hits. Don't worry about getting attacked by the men. They have melee attacks and a diagonal charge strike, but Shifu is far too strong. They'll do next to no damage, allowing you to freely wail on them.

After the fight, the men will realise who the Shifu is. They'll apologise and run away from the Earthern Heart master, allowing him to talk with the woman's grandson. He'll apologise for robbing Shifu and return the money. Before Shifu can leave, he'll ask whether he can become Shifu's disciple.

Shifu leans towards refusing (although you can accept at this point as well). However, if you do refuse, we'll meet the grandson again at the base of Mount Aspiration. There, you can also accept his request to become a disciple. He'll reveal his name is Yuan Jou and join the party.

Returning to the Peak of Mount Aspiration

With all three disciples in tow, it's time to head back up Mount Aspiration. Return to the path and climb the steps we used to reach the base of the mountain.

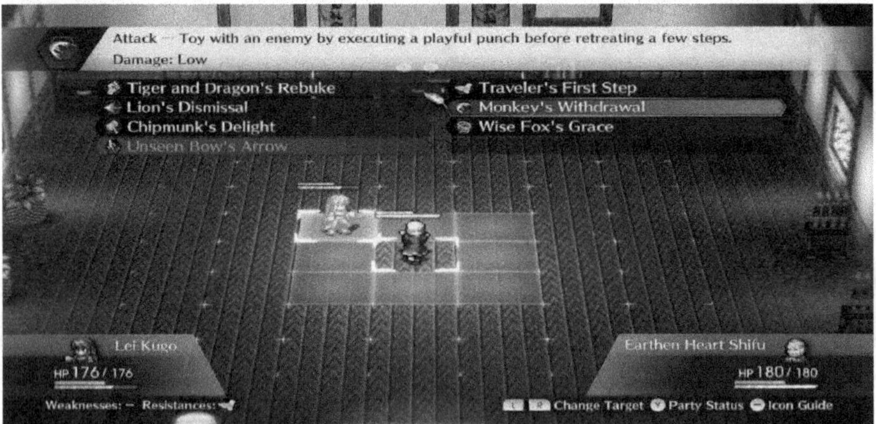

Once you shift screens to the second layer of Mount Aspiration, enter Shifu's Cottage. Inside, we'll watch a scene where he chats to his three students about Earthen Heart. After a brief discussion, we'll have to fight all three disciples individually. Unless you spent time raising each recruit's level, these should be fairly straightforward fights. Lei will start. Hit Wise Fox's Grace. She'll likely hit you with a melee attack, but it'll do very little damage and you'll bind her. Follow up with two Lion's Dismissals and she'll go down.

Hong is next. The same strategy is employed here. Hit him with Wise Fox's Grace. Hong has a lot more health than Lei, but you can basically stun-lock him using a mixture of Tiger & Dragon's Rebuke and Traveler's First Step. His melee attacks are slow, and should miss Shifu most of the time.

Finally, it's Yuan's turn. Yuan is arguably the biggest pushover of all three fighters, with the least experience. You know the strategy by now. Hit him with Wise Fox's Grace. Once he's bound, use Chipmunk's Delight and he should be down for the count.

Once he's defeated, the scene will move on to Shifu's Cottage at night, with the master celebrating finding so many promising disciples in such a short amount of time.

Training

Right, let's talk training. From here on in, we basically have to pick who's going to inherit the Earthen Heart. The game won't flat out ask us, but our strongest pupil will gain the honour, so we'll have to focus on turning one student into a badass. That entails beating them up until they level up and learn new skills.

So, which one should you pick? Well, honestly it's a matter of preference. Each has unique stats, but will deliver adequately if you opt to entrust them with the legacy of Earthern Heart. Let's run through the playstyle of each disciple:

Hong - Hong is essentially your tank class, possessing a high Defense and Attack stat. He's very useful in melee situations.

Lei - Lei has high Speed but low Attack. She's best used when dipping in and out of fights, as you can smartly position her to take down enemies without getting hit.

Yuan - Yuan is something of a middle ground between Hong and Lei. His Attack and Speed aren't bad, however, his Defense is low, meaning he's susceptible to big attacks.

Day 1

Once you've chosen your star pupil, opt to spend all your time training with them. On the first day, that'll come in the form of Stamina training.

You'll be able to go four rounds, increasing your opponent's Physical Defence stat by 5 each time and awarding them EXP. Focus all your training on one pupil.

You've already fought all of these pupils during the previous section of this chapter and the strategies remain the same.

Generally, hit your chosen disciple with Wise Fox's Grace and beat them down with your other abilities until they fall. Once the first stint of battles is over, your disciple should've reached level 7.

Day 2

Day 2 will take place in Bamboo Forest, with Shifu focusing on the Speed stat. Head over to your pupil and grind out all four battles.

There's a good chance your disciple may be getting a little tougher at this point, so if you need a good strategy to reliably win battles, lure them to the centre, stand on a tile diagonal to them and hit Lion's Dismissal. This will knock them back.

If you get in a good loop, you can keep knocking your opponent back and forcing them to use their turn to reposition before hitting them with the same move again. It's a good way to chip off health without taking any punishment.

Each round during day 2 will strengthen your pupil's Speed stat by 5. Rinse out all four battles to officially end your training stint in the Bamboo Forest. Your pupil should be around level 8 at this point.

Day 3

You know the drill by now. Head to your disciple and engage them in battle. Maintain the strategy from before and you should be able to take your opponent down. Each time you do, they'll gain five Physical Attack stat.

After four battles, the day will come to an end. We'll then cut to a short scene of Shifu and the pupils training before we reach the group's final lesson. Just before Shifu can deliver the lesson, the shopkeeper from Yunfa Market will burst through the doors, calling on Shifu to help the town thwart a bandit attack.

Dealing With The bandits

Once you regain control, descend the mountain and head for Yunfa Market. It's the same place we found Hong stealing noodles earlier in the chapter. Once you arrive, head to the top of the street and talk to the group of gang members.

These are the same bandits that you fought while recruiting Yun earlier, although they'll claim this time they've been training.

All that training won't do much though. After a short conversation, a battle will begin.

Stand to the right of each bandit and hit Monkey's Withdrawal. The weaker bandits will go down in one or two hits from the attack (they're vulnerable to it).

Don't worry too much about getting in their line of fire, as their melee and ranged moves are still fairly weak.

Their leader is a little more powerful, although the tactic is the same. Hit Monkey's Withdrawal until he falls.

After the fight, the bandits will flee, telling Shifu that Ou Di Wan Lee will take him and his school down.

Seems we have the name of the bandit leader. After you regain control, speak to the girls surrounding Shifu. They'll give you a Panda Charm, a Chow Chow Charm and a Peach Bun.

Head down the street but be sure to talk to every single person you see on the way. Each one has a gift to show you their appreciation, ranging from food and accessories to armour. After you've spoken to them all, leave Yunfa Market.

The Attack on Aspiration Mountain

After leaving Yunfa Market, return to the base of Aspiration Mountain and scale it. Once you arrive at Shifu's Cottage, you'll find the place has been attacked. You'll find the two disciples you didn't train dead, and your star pupil gravely wounded nearby.

After speaking to your living trainee, you'll cut to a funeral for the two deceased pupils, with Shifu showing his disciple his most prized possession: an incredibly powerful move known as Heavenly Peaks Descent. He tells them this move isn't one they'll be able to execute just yet, but eventually, he hopes to see them carry on the legacy of the ability.

The scene will then cut back to the cottage. Shifu will tell the pupil to rest while he pays respect to the fallen. However, he's actually secretly preparing to go full John Wick and settle one final score.

Indomitable Fist Fortress

Once we regain control, head down to the base of Aspiration Mountain and towards Bamboo Forest. We went there earlier when we recruited Lei.

Follow the path through Bamboo Forest until you reach a fork in the road. If Lei was the survivor of the bandit massacre, she'll join you here. Take the central path and continue following it.

You'll arrive at the Indomitable Fist Fortress. Head towards the doors and talk to the two guards.

You'll initiate a fight with the guards. Use Monkey's Withdrawal on both of them to kill them instantly, ending the fight. Once the fight's done, we'll see a cutscene of a young boy confronting the clan of the Indomitable Fist, attempting to use a powerful move that backfires. He'll flee, leaving the doors wide open for Shifu. If Yun was your trainee, he'll join the fight here.

Head inside and you'll enter a fight with a whopping 9 bandits. You know the drill. Back up and use Monkey's Withdrawal to finish your foes. You'll probably get punished a lot by the bandits, but Shifu's resistant to their main Top Knot and Flurry melee attacks, which should allow you to tank a fair few hits. Regardless, if you need to heal, make a hole in their attack formation and flee to the bottom tiles to use a healing item.

When they're finished, approach the leader north of where Shifu's stood. He's slightly stronger than the standard grunts but the same strategy applies; hit him with Monkey's Withdrawal. Once he's done, head up the steps to your right or left. Several goons will appear on the steps, releasing two white tigers that run to Shifu.

Take them both on. They're weak to Traveler's First Step and won't do huge melee damage, so position yourself diagonally to them and lay in the kicks. They should go down quickly. Take down the two goons who released the tigers and their leader, then head through the doors north of you.

Two goons will run up to you once you enter the palace, finish them off with some well-placed Monkey's Withdrawal and loot the pots to their left. You'll find a Fuxi Feather, a Red Bean Bun and a pair of Weathered Boots. Proceed through the curtain north of you and then through a second curtain at the back of the room. You'll arrive in a long corridor. Head right until you encounter a tiger. Defeat it using Traveller's First Step and then continue following the corridor to the right.

You'll find another curtain at the end of the corridor. Head through and you'll wind up in a room with two goons. Defeat them with Monkey's Withdrawal and loot the pots to the right. You should find a Peach Bun. Next, loot the cupboard at the back right-hand side of the room for a pair of Qilin Boots. Push through the north curtain and you'll enter another room with two goons and a leader. Take all three out.

Head to the back of the room. You'll find a tea set to your right and three pots to your left. Examine all four items. You'll get a Soup Dumpling and 2 Peach Buns. Proceed through the northern door and you'll be faced with five leaders. This is a tougher fight than taking on general grunts, so it's best to use a move that can hit all your foes. Let's position ourselves in the middle of the group and use Wise Fox's Grace. It'll hit everyone one tile away from us, which will make short work of the group.

You might have to take a moment to heal here, as the five enemies can hit hard as a unit. When you need to stock up, retreat and use one of the various items you've likely stored up to this point. After the fight's done, continue down the corridor until you see a curtain. Enter it and you'll find yourself in a room with a tiger. Defeat it and push through the curtain north of you.

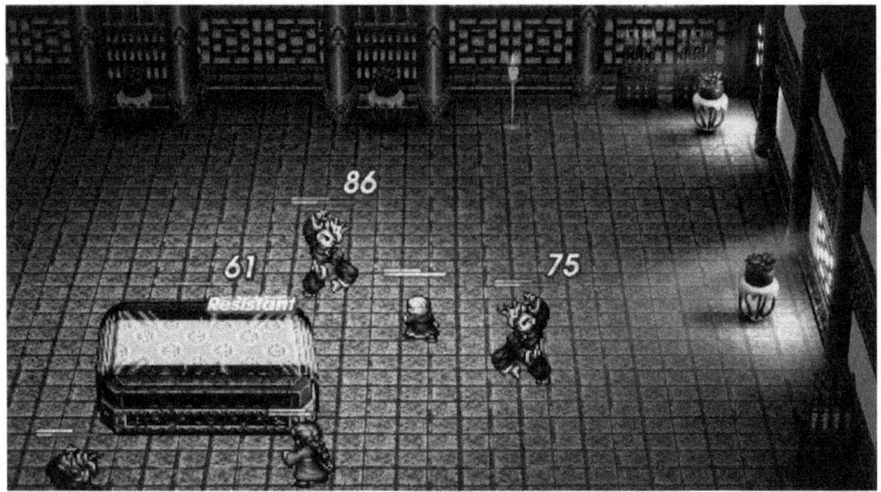

You'll enter a room filled with warriors. If Hong was your star pupil, he'll join the party here. From this point forward, all players should have their surviving disciple as backup. Engage the 5 warriors in battle. These guys are tough, but nothing you haven't faced before. Have Shifu and his pupil use Lion's Dismissal against the group (they're vulnerable to the attack), while also relying on Wise Fox's Grace when surrounded to hit several foes at once.

After the battle, head to the top left-hand corner and search the two pots. One will contain a Bottle Gourd and the other a Pork Bun. With those looted, head through the curtains north of your position. You'll enter a long corridor with a tiger and two grunts. You'll have to fight all three enemies at once. Hit the grunts with Monkey's Withdrawal and the tiger with Traveller's First Step.

Once they're down, proceed through the curtain ahead. You'll enter a giant room with a large table running through its centre. Here, we'll meet Ou Di Wan Lee, head of the Indomitable Fist. He'll tell us that we have to defeat his 12 disciples before we can challenge him. Equip Shifu and your pupil with the best gear you have. We're about to throw down.

The Revelry of Blood

The rules of this challenge are simple. Shifu and his student have to approach each set of combatants one at a time, defeating them to advance to the next stage. In total, there are six fights here, with each battle growing increasingly difficult. One tip to make things easier: save between every fight. None of them should give you too much trouble, but making a mistake and slipping up could cost you dearly if you haven't saved since the beginning of the trial.

Once you're stocked up with equipment, let's take on the first pairing: San Xi and Su Xi. Approach either of the fighters (they're the first pairing at the table) and the battle will begin.

Battle 1: San Xi and Su Xi

This fight should be the easiest of the bunch. San Xi (the warrior in yellow) is weak to Monkey's Withdrawal, so hit him with that to inflict big damage.

His partner, Su Xi (the warrior in blue) is only weak to one move Shifu has in his arsenal: Unseen Bow's Arrow. Annoyingly, Shifu can only use this move as a ranged counter, so we'll just have to make sure to pack in the damage with moves he's not resistant to. That makes Traveler's First Step, Lion's Dismissal, Chipmunk's Delight, Monkey's Withdrawal and Wise Fox's Grace useful attacks to take him down.

Neither fighter will do much damage, so don't worry about tanking hits to take them both down quickly and efficiently.

Battle 2: Yi Xi and Er Xi

Once they're done, it's time for battle number 2, this time against Yi Xi and Er Xi. Approach them to kick off the bout. Yi Xi (the warrior in red) is weak to Agile attacks, so Traveler's First Step is our go-to if we want to take him down. He has a wind attack, but it won't do much to either Shifu or his pupil.

Meanwhile, Er Xi (the warrior in green) is weak to punches, meaning Tiger and Dragon's Rebuke is our best bet at carving off chunks of his health. Seeing as Tiger and Dragon's Rebuke is a low-damage attack, you can also just rely on Wise Fox's Grace, which will inflict a lot of damage. Er Xi has a melee attack that knocks an opponent back, but he isn't able to get much offense off if you're pressuring him.

Once they're down, it's time for the next pair of fighters.

Battle 3: Tong Cha and Sha Cha

After the battle begins, let's immediately head towards Tong Cha (the fighter in the red jacket). He's vulnerable to Lion's Dismissal, so let's take him down with that. Hit the move as both Shifu and his student until Tong Cha is finished.

Once one Cha is down, the other will likely charge up a melee attack that can hit several tiles in front of him, so if you see his red charge bar fill up, move down several tiles or attempt to interrupt him by hitting him. Assuming Tong Cha (the fighter in the blue jacket) is left, let's deal with him. Technically he's weak to Monkey Withdrawal, but his health is so high that you're best to hit him with a move that does at least medium damage. Use Wise Fox's Grace to take him down quickly. Once he's done, the battle will end.

Battle 4: Pei Cha and Nan Cha

Let's move on to our fourth battle, this time against Pei Cha and Nan Cha. Pei Cha (the warrior in the yellow jacket) is weak to fire, which we don't have. Instead, the best idea is to simply hit him with moves like Wise Fox's Grace and Lion's Dismissal as Shifu, and any of your student's abilities that do medium, high or massive damage.

Like last time, the death of the first Cha will inspire the second to wind up a hard-hitting melee strike. Make sure to knock him out of the attack or move Shifu and his student out of the way to dodge the blow. Once the remaining Cha has executed the attack (or been interrupted), move in to fight him. If the remaining attacker is Nan Cha (the warrior in the black jacket), we'll technically want to Martial attacks, as he's weak to them.

However, much like in the last fight, it's better to rely on strikes with medium or high damage considering Nan Cha has a high health pool. Considering Nan Cha is resistant to Wise Fox's Grace, our best bet is to rely on our student's pool of moves to take him down. Find something with medium or strong damage and wail on Nan Cha. Once he's down, the fight will move on.

Battle 5: Lin, Xian and Chia

After listening to Ou Di Wan Lee taunt us, it's time for our fifth battle, this time against three sisters. Much like the battles before, each sister has her own stats, weaknesses and strengths. Xian (the sister with two maces) is weak to kicks, Lin (the sister with two swords) isn't weak to anything and Chan (the sister with the staff) is weak to water.

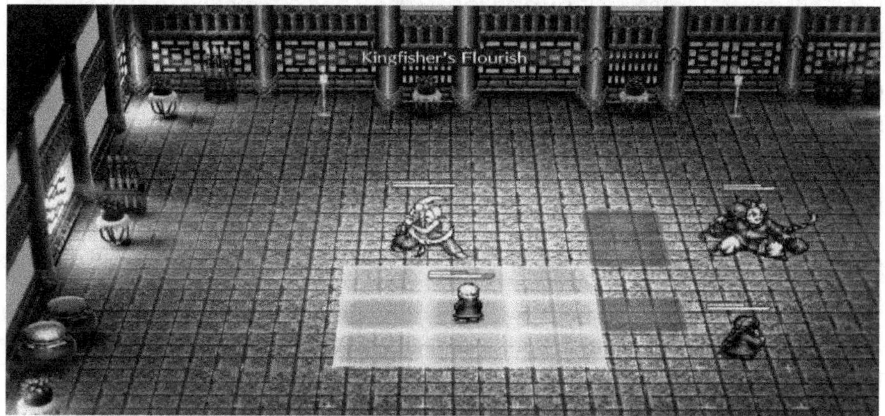

Our main tactic here is to separate and take down each sister individually. Together, their attacks can be overwhelming.

However, if we divide and conquer, Shifu and his student can pack in enough damage to take down each sister quickly without them doing too much damage. Move quickly and position your fighters so that your target is body blocking their allies.

Let's start with Chan. She has a spin attack that allows her to move across the board quickly, so nixing her from the offset cuts off any ranged potential. She also has a ranged fire attack that we want to avoid.

If you can, get behind her or use a spin attack so she's facing away. Once you're in position, use Wise Fox's Grace or any other medium/high damage attack to take her down quickly. She'll still be able to hit combatants standing behind her, but her attacks will do less damage.

Next, let's take down Xian. She's the only sister with a weakness we can exploit. Head to Xian's position and hit her with Traveler's First Step.

Xian has a melee attack that can hit twice, but it shouldn't do too much damage. Just make sure to have both fighters corner her and lay in the attacks. Once she's down, let's finish the fight.

With just Lin left, it should be easier to lay in big attacks. Close the distance and hit her with any medium or high damage moves. As Lin doesn't have a weakness, we really just need to inflict as much damage as possible.

If you can, stay behind her. Her melee attack doesn't do a lot of base damage, but it hits several times, so it's worth respecting it and attempting to stay out of its way.

Once she's done, we'll advance to the final bracket of Ou Di Wan Lee's challenge. Save the game and let's get ready to face the old man on the right-hand side of the table.

Battle 6: Yi Pei Kou

As you approach Ou Di Wan Lee, he'll initiate the final fight against the old man at the end of the table.

Yi Pei Kou is the top henchman here and the only thing standing between us and his dastardly master.

Much like Lin in the last fight, Kou has no weaknesses. He is, however, strong to pretty much every single physical attack, meaning most of Shifu and his student's move set will do reduced damage. One of the only attacks he isn't strong against is Wise Fox's Grace, so that's Shifu's move of choice going forward. Meanwhile, if your student has any moves with medium or high damage that Kou isn't weak to, that's their go-to pick. Otherwise, they'll also rely on Wise Fox's Grace.

As for Yi Pei Kou, he has a close-range melee attack that can bind Shifu and his pupil. This move will deal a moderate amount of damage, but if you're playing it smart, you should be able to tank the hits without much repercussion. The only problem is Kou's ability to bind prevents you from using certain attacks when it lands. To make matters worse, if you retreat while trying to let this status ailment wear off, Kou can land a ranged charge attack.

Your best bet is to stay behind him and land weak blows until bind has worn off, or use the other combatant as bait while you wait. Before long, Kou will fall and the battle will end. Save the game and prepare for our final fight.

Point of No Return Warning

With Kou down, this is our point of no return warning. Any items you want to find in the palace or anywhere else throughout Imperial China's map, now's the time to do it. We'll also want to load all our best equipment onto the pupil (or remove it from Shifu and add it back to the inventory). It'll come in handy during the Final Chapter. Once you're ready, let's do this.

Ou Di Wan Lee Fight

After the final bracket fight is done, approach Ou Di Wan Lee. He'll summon two bodyguards, who surround Shifu and his pupil. Just as all hope seems lost, Shifu will tell his pupil that he'll hold off the bodyguards while they fight Ou Di Wan Lee. The pupil will object but Shifu will tell them they're powerful enough. All they have to do is use Heavenly Peaks Descent: the move Shifu performed on the mountain.

The pupil will jump on the table and challenge Ou Di Wan Lee. Once Ou Di Wan Lee jumps on the table to battle them, the pupil will remember the teachings of Heavenly Peaks Descent and it'll be added to their ability list. Our final battle will then begin.

The battle will be between our surviving pupil and Ou Di Wan Lee. As soon as it starts, hit Heavenly Peaks Descent. It hits three tiles above, below, to the right, to the left and diagonal of the pupil. This should knock down around half of Ou Di Wan Lee's health bar. We won't be able to hit it again in the battle (it's a one-time deal for now), but that should help us even the odds.

Now for the rest of the fight. Ou Di Wan Lee has no weaknesses or resistances, so our game plan from here on in is to just whittle away his health with our strongest attacks. Ou Di Wan Lee will rely on a ranged poison attack at a distance, which hits for low damage but leaves the pupil poisoned until they either heal or the fight concludes.

What you really want to watch out for is Mad Dragon's Vengeance, which he can pull out of nowhere. It hits for 150 damage or more. It's nigh on unavoidable unless we're directly next to Ou Di, so let's do that. Be warned though; Ou Di's favourite close quarters move (Rabid Wolf's Rage) knocks you back a few tiles, setting up Mad Dragon's Vengeance.

Make sure to close the gap again as fast as possible whenever he hits it. Get in close and hit as many powerful moves as you can. Focus on abilities doing medium or high damage. Make sure to heal whenever you need to. We should have plenty of food by this point, including restoratives like the Peach Bun that heal the poison status ailment.

Once he's done, we'll see the student straight up send Ou Di Wan Lee into the shadow realm with a monstrous roundhouse kick. They'll then attend to Shifu, who's close to death. He'll tell the student he's proud of them and pass away. We'll then cut to the top of Mount Aspiration, as the student trains. Congratulations, you have preserved the legacy of Earthen Heart. Time to pick a new character.

Twilight of Edo Japan

Sent away on a seemingly impossible mission, Live A Live's Twilight of Edo Japan chapter sees a young shinobi defying the odds and embarking on the quest of a lifetime. He'll have to infiltrate a castle, save a trapped prisoner and defeat a corrupt lord while battling demons, samurais and everything in between.

The walkthrough below will show you how best to navigate this non-linear chapter, including how to find two secret bosses, an optional companion and some hard-to-find equipment.

Looking for a specific section of the chapter? Skip between each section using the links below:

The Twilight of Edo Japan

The chapter will open with two dramatic cutscenes. The first will show an evil lord speaking to his three magical subjects, learning that he's managed to capture an important prisoner. After hearing from all three of his minions, the lord will claim that war is coming to Japan.

We'll then cut to a second cutscene, this time depicting a shinobi master sending his inexperienced pupil to complete a seemingly impossible mission. Speaking of this inexperienced pupil, you'll now get to name them.

Pick something out or stick with the shinobi's default name: Oboromaru (which is what we'll be calling him in this walkthrough).

After you've named your new protagonist, he'll drop from the ceiling and begin talking with the master shinobi. We'll be asked whether we want to hear the details once more. You can select "yes" to skip the explanation or "I would hear them again" if you need a quick brief of your mission.

To recap in case you skipped the description, our mission is to head to Lord Ode Lou's castle and rescue a captive being held in the dungeons. Our master reveals that how we reach this captive and free him really is up to us. We can senselessly murder the Ode clan or act as a shadow, sneaking through unseen. Regardless, we must be successful.

Once we're done talking to the master, Hayate will teach us a new ability: Shadowed Self. It will allow us to blend into the environment by pressing Y. With that learnt, Oboromaru will leave the room to begin his mission.

Ground Rules

We'll cut to Oboromaru arriving at the castle. There are a few things to note here. First, Oboromaru has a map which you can access at any time by pressing the minus button. Secondly, there are three different ways to approach this chapter: lethally, non-lethally or a mix of the two.

If you want to play non-lethally, it's worth noting that killing demons, monsters or anything non-human doesn't count towards the kill number. You'll receive a special reward for accomplishing this feat, although it's tough to ensure that count stays at zero so keep a lot of saves to walk back on an accidental kill.

As for lethal players, there are 100 enemies to kill in this section, with Oboromaru keeping count as you play. If you want to hit that number, you can't kill any of the women you encounter until the very end of the chapter (unless they're demons). As you're about to face the final boss, you'll meet a secret NPC if all women are spared. Once she's dead, you'll then have to return and kill all of the NPCs you spared to reach 100 kills.

Infiltrating The Castle

Once you gain control, you'll find yourself on a path leading towards a large settlement. Push forward. You'll arrive at a gate patrolled by two guards. If you aren't bothered about taking lives, approach them and take them down. However, it's a good idea to get used to the Shadowed Self ability here.

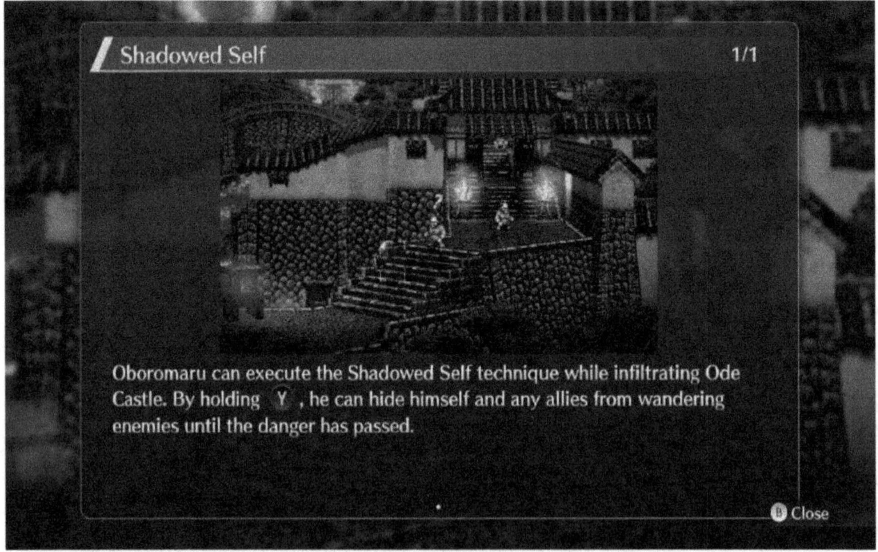

If you walk toward the guards, an exclamation mark will appear above their heads. Press Y to use Shadowed Self and render Oboromaru invisible. They'll lose sight of you.

Wait for a few seconds and eventually question marks will appear above their head. This indicates the guards are now searching. They'll move around the area looking for you. Wait for them to face away and run through the centre.

If you do wind up fighting them, these guards shouldn't pose much of a problem. They're incredibly weak to fire and will likely fall from Oboromaru's Shadow Slash ability. So position yourself smartly, and you should be able to dispatch them with ease.

However you passed through the previous area, you'll now enter a second guard-patrolled courtyard. Use the same technique to sneak past them or take them down. Either way, let's head through the set of double doors in front of us.

Passwords

Inside the building ahead, a cutscene will play, with Oboromaru heading towards a screen and crouching next to it. He'll hear a group of guards being assembled by a general. The general will shout "password" and they'll shout back "River". Meanwhile, one of the guards will shout potato and get dragged off (Sasha Braus would've had a REAL tough time working here...). Evidently, the punishment is severe for giving the wrong password.

Oboromaru will note that Hayate told him that the passwords were "River" and "Origin". From now on, if you hear a loud bell ring, the password switches between these two phrases.

Right now, the password is River, so keep an ear out for the bell as that will change. Don't worry too much about forgetting the password, as Oboromaru will note which one it's switched to whenever the bell rings.

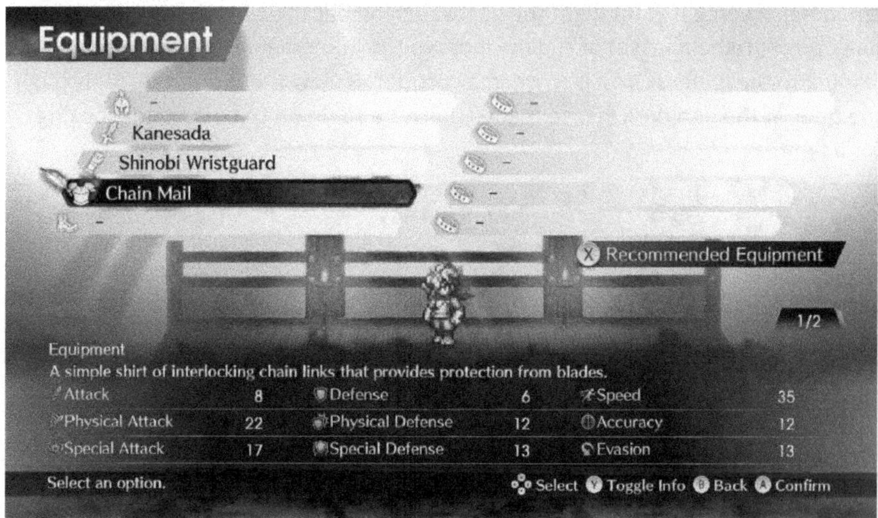

Continue forward into the hallway ahead. There are three doors we can take here. First, let's head through the sliding door on the right-hand side of the hallway. Inside, you'll find a soldier and a chest. If you aren't afraid of getting your hands dirty, kill the soldier. Otherwise, use shadowed self to sneak around him to the top left-hand side of the room. Inside the chest, you'll find Chainmail Armour, which you can equip in the equipment menu.

Leave the room and head back to the centre of the corridor. If you're aiming for a lethal run, head through the sliding door in the centre. You'll reach a room with the general we saw giving orders earlier. Approach him and he'll initiate a fight. This general is a trickier battle than the general grunts we'll find throughout the temple, with a brutal melee strike he'll deliver to opponents in a one-tile radius and a charge attack that can hit you for huge damage early on if you're diagonal to him.

The easiest technique in these early battles is to rely on Oboromaru's fire powers. Use Fireflies' Wake and make sure the general is in the blast. Once it's landed, it'll lay a set of fire tiles on the floor. Put a lot of space between yourself and your opponent. He'll continue to take fire damage if he's stood in the fire tiles, eventually dying if you can keep the chase going long enough. Just make sure you aren't standing diagonally from him to avoid the charge attack and he should fall fairly quickly.

Once he's down, you'll get the Top Knot armour piece which you can equip in the equipment menu. If you fought the general, head back to the corridor. Now, let's head through the final set of sliding doors to the immediate left of the doors leading to the general. You'll arrive in a corridor. Follow it but don't head through the door at the end until you're ready. There's a ronin on the other side looking for a fight.

If you're playing non-lethal, use shadowed self to sneak past. Otherwise, approach the ronin and prepare for a fight. Ronins are one of the weaker enemy types found throughout Ode's fortress. Use fire attacks to keep them at bay and don't stand diagonal to them, as it allows them to unleash a charge attack.

Once he's done, we'll have two options. The non-lethal squad will want to head through the door to the north of where the ronin was standing. Lethal-squad want to head south of where he was standing. Follow the route until you enter a small room with a guard and a maid.

For those wanting maximum kills, take down the guard but leave the maid. We'll come back for her at the end of the chapter. Now, head into the ronin corridor and continue through the door to the north to rejoin paths with the non-lethal crew.

You'll enter a courtyard. Up the stairs ahead, you'll find a ronin patrolling. Kill him for the lethal side and sneak past for the non-lethal. Continue along the path and you'll run into a second ronin. Once again, either kill or sneak past him depending on your playstyle. When you reach the end of the path, you'll find a set of double doors guarded by two grunts. They'll ask you for the password. If the bell hasn't chimed, it'll be "River". If it has chimed, then it'll be "Origin".

The bell will continuously chime from here on out, so you'll need to keep on top of which password is correct. If you can't remember, just wait around until the password changes and Oboromaru comments on it.

If you want the most lethal playthrough, answer the guards with the wrong password. You'll enter a fight scenario where you can kill them. Lethal players will also want to hang left of the guarded doors and make their way around the building until they see a hiding spot with light protruding from it. It's just next to a bush with red flowers. You'll be able to speak to a merchant hiding here who you can kill to raise your body count.

Regardless of whether you're on a killing spree or a stealthy infiltration, push ahead into the palace beyond the double doors. When inside, enter the sliding doors ahead. A ronin will be patrolling the hallway you arrive in. Kill him if you're playing lethally. If you aren't, let's strategize which path we're going down.

Residential Palace, Main Corridor

From here, things become a little confusing. The Residential Palace has several paths and there are enemies, loot and lore to be found down each. Namely, we'll have four different routes stemming from this main corridor, so let's cover what's through each one.

Sliding doors on the far left

The sliding doors on the far left will lead you to a second small corridor with three doors. The door on the right leads to the back of the palace (it's the same corridor we reach by using the sliding doors on the left).

Meanwhile, the central door leads to an encounter with a minister. Don't bother going in here if you're opting for a non-lethal showdown.

As for the lethal crew, this minister will spawn two shinobis when you enter. This can be a tough fight (potentially too tough for your level, meaning you should come back here after you've gained a bit more experience).

If you do decide to tough it out though, the best tactic is to position Oboromaru so that he can use Firefall on both shinobis at once, knocking down their health pools significantly over the course of the fight.

You'll want to stay close to both enemies, as their melee strikes are actually far less brutal than their ranged blows.

When they fall, turn your attention to the Minister. Talk to him and kill him in the encounter to add him to your kill counter. If you want, you can use the hidden passage in the top right-hand corner of the room to access the attic from here, although we'll go to the attic shortly regardless.

Once you're done in this room (if you went in at all), return to the corridor and talk to the ronin on the left-hand side of the corridor. He'll ask for the password. Give it to him to access the room ahead or give him the wrong password and defeat him to add him to the kill counter. For now, you won't find anything in here. Although, once you return from the attic, (presuming you peeked through the hole on the east side of the area) a couple will enter the room. If they're in the room, leave them be for the time being.

After you've investigated each room, return to the main corridor.

Sliding doors on the left

This door leads to a corridor of maids. We aren't going to kill anyone down here just yet, so push past and you'll wind up in another short corridor leading to the palace's exit. Let's not head through the exit just yet. Instead, take a right and enter the south door on the far right-hand side of the room.

Inside, you'll find two chests. They both contain Castella Cake, which is sure to help us out down the line. With our pockets filled with cake, head back to the main corridor.

Sliding doors on the right

Through the sliding doors in the centre, you'll find a ronin and another general to take down if you're playing lethally. Luckily, we won't need to take them on together. Approach the ronin and he'll initiate a fight. Kill him and, once the battle's over, you'll be stood face to face with the general.

Before fighting the general, there's something to keep in mind. If we kill him prior to entering the attic, we'll miss a cutscene and an item. So it's wiser to leave him until after we've explored the attic. If you've already been up there (or don't care about getting the item), slay him, otherwise, we'll come back in a bit.

Sliding doors on the far right

Through the sliding doors on the right, you'll find a merchant. Kill him if you're playing lethally or walk past him if you're playing non-lethally. In the back-left-hand corner of the room, you'll see a wooden panel with a small engraving at the bottom. This is one of several fake wall panels we'll find throughout the chapter.

Walk towards it to access a secret room. Inside, you'll meet a rival shinobi asking for a password. Non-lethal players will want to give him the correct password; lethal players will want to give the wrong password, initiating a fight.

Once this shinobi's done, you'll gain access to a ladder leading to the attic. There are a few things to find here, including some holes you can peek through to gain useful information. Arguably the most important slice of info is that there's a key hidden in the store room. We can also find a chest in the southmost part of the attic (it contains Castella Cake) and a second chest containing Suijin Tabi shoes by the ladder in the east part of the attic.

If you didn't kill the general through the sliding doors on the right in the main corridor, you'll also see a cutscene where a thief and his son attempting to steal from the Ode clan. The thief will be killed by the general and his son will drag him away. If we see this cutscene, we'll be able to find a Koban from one of the chests the thief was attempting to steal from.

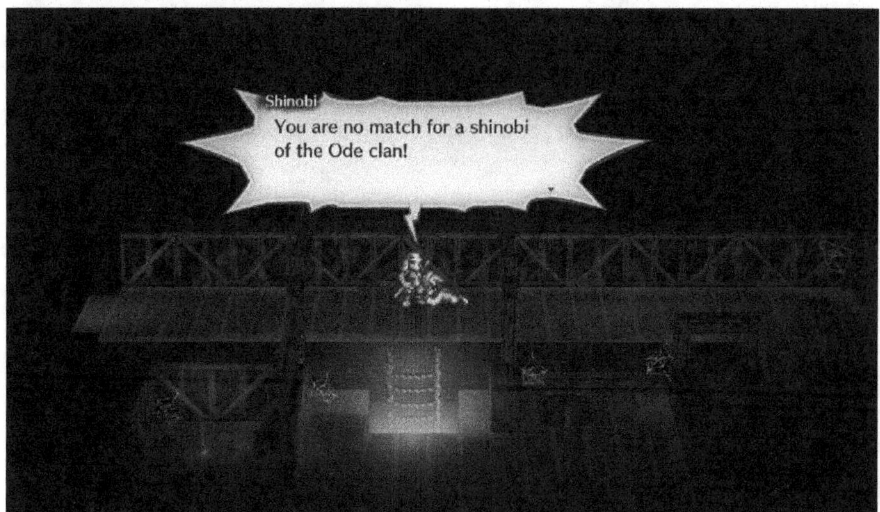

If you head towards the path leading out of the back of the attic, a shinobi will appear, initiating a fight. Kill him if you're playing lethal; flee if you're playing non-lethal.

How to Get The Storehouse Key

If you're ready to move on, head through the passage behind the shinobi. We'll find ourselves on the exterior walls surrounding the compound. Once you've emerged, follow the wall south. Eventually, you'll reach a small tower with a ladder. If you're playing non-lethally, don't head up here. There's a battle coming up that's impossible to flee from. If you're playing lethally, climb the ladder, and head into one of the hidden openings on either side of the tower.

You'll enter a crawlspace. Crawl forward and five shinobis will appear. Initially, this may seem like an overwhelming battle. However, every shinobi except for the leader of the pack is actually an illusion. You can wipe them all out by targeting the shinobi in the back left-hand corner. Just keep your distance and use Firefall. If you're getting ragged on by his allies, use a Shrimp Rice Ball to restore your health.

If you're successful, you'll access the Kotetsu sword and get a Fuma Shuriken. The Kotetsu sword will raise your attack by 8, making it a useful tool for a lethal playstyle. After the battle's done, head to the two chests at the back of the room to get a Genji Glove and a Koban.

Leave the crawlspace, descend the ladder and continue following the wall east. You'll enter a room with a large false panel in its centre (a rat will run on it and fall to the room below, indicating it's a fake). Proceed around this panel and out of the exit on the opposite side. You'll arrive back on the wall. Continue following it.

Eventually, you'll reach a wooden outcrop you can use to drop down to the garden below. Let's not take this route just yet. Instead, continue following the wall until you enter another crawlspace. Just next to the entrance to this area, you'll find three chests. In the central chest in the Storehouse Key.

Let's go ahead and use this key now. Backtrack across the wall all the way to the Residental Palace attic, returning to the corridor with the four doors we were in earlier. Head south, leaving through the entrance to the Residential Palace. If we descend the steps southeast from the Residental Palace entrance, we'll reach a locked doorway.

Use the Storeroom Key to enter the doors. Inside, we'll find the Shinobi Storehouse. Approach the chest south of the entrance and you'll find the Dungeon Key inside. However, be warned. You'll have to battle an onslaught of shinobis directly after accessing this chest, so save before accessing it. If you're playing non-lethally, use Shadowed Self and make a beeline for the entrance.

If you're playing lethally and want to kill the shinobis who call this safehouse home, you'll battle three waves of enemies. The first wave consists of one shinobi, the second wave consists of two shinobis and then the final wave pits you against four shinobis. The first two battles shouldn't be too difficult. However, the fourth can be rough, especially as the shinobis can execute their attacks back to back. The best tactic is to use Firefall or an ability with long-range and position yourself so you're hitting them all at once. Don't be afraid to heal or flee if things are getting too tricky; you can always come back.

Spirit Storehouse

Once you're done in this room, head back to the Residential Palace. When in the corridor with four doors, head through the door on the left leading to the hallway of maids. Follow it to the end and, when reaching the short corridor on the other side, exit the Residential Palace through the double doors ahead of you. When you emerge, head right when facing the stone archway, crossing the nearby bridge. At the end of the path, you'll find a set of double doors.

They'll be locked, but you can use the Storeroom Key to unlock them. Before we enter, note down the location of this room.

It'll be crucial to levelling up a bit later in this level, as the spirits inside this Storehouse respawn when you leave and re-enter the area.

Once you do head inside, you'll find a woman and three spirits (they look like blue flames). Touching a spirit will start a battle encounter.

These spirits are weak and incredibly vulnerable to fire, so you shouldn't have too many issues fighting them.

Head up the steps and loot the five chests on the right (they'll contain some armour, Koban and scrolls) as well as the two pots on the left (they'll both contain food).

It's worth noting that fighting spirits and the woman in the corner won't count towards your kill tally.

It means non-lethal players can prep themselves for tough battles in here, gaining some levels to help combat the area's tougher demonic enemies.

When you're ready, talk to the woman in the top left-hand corner of the area. She'll fight you, not allowing you to flee until she's been vanquished.

Much like the multiple shinobi fight earlier in the mission, there are five combatants here (the woman and four candle sticks that spew flames), but the battle solely relies on you taking out the mysterious woman. Focus your attacks on her, and she should go down in no time.

Once she's dead and you're ready to move on, leave the storeroom. We can technically head down the tree to the left of the storeroom doors and enter the stronghold through its main entrance, but let's opt for the more secretive infiltration route.

Path of Shuttered Lanterns

Head back to the Residential Palace attic, through the exit at the back left-hand corner of the room, and then follow the wall south.

Once you've navigated through the crawlspace with the fake floor, continue following the wall until you reach the small wooden outcrop we passed on our way to get the Storeroom Key earlier.

Use it to navigate down to the garden below and then interact with the large steel lantern south of where you land. It'll expose a path leading down. Open it and head inside to access the Path of Shuttered Lanterns. There's an optional boss in this corridor, although it's way too tricky for us right now, so we'll come back to it in a bit.

For now, continue down this passageway. As you enter the second corridor, you'll notice Oboromaru briefly stop twice as two clicking sounds play. Ignore that for now, as we'll come back to it shortly.

Castle Keep Moat

Exit the corridor and you'll find yourself standing at the bottom of the fortress' moat. Enter the water and Oboromaru will begin swimming. Look out for small wooden pipes poking out of the water.

These are enemies. If you touch one, you'll initiate a battle with a shinobi. There should be two in the lower section of the moat. Unfortunately for the non-lethal crew, you'll not be able to use Shadowed Self when underwater, so we'll have to rely on evading enemies the old-fashioned way.

Navigate to the left side of the screen until you see stairs leading to a small wooden firepit and a tree. Make your way to the tree and ascend it to reach the next section of the moat. Before we press on, let's make note of a particularly tricky enemy lurking here. The black blob roaming the water without a wooden pipe above it is a secret boss that we are currently much too weak to face. Note its position and evade it.

Once past it, you'll find another submerged shinobi to evade or fight. Defeat or evade him and follow the moat north until you find a door leading to the second floor of the Castle Dungeon. Enter the door and ascend the stairs. You'll arrive in a corridor with two cells.

If you're playing lethal, take down the Retainer in the centre of the hallway. The best method (if you have it) is to rely on Phantom Butterflies, which deals heavy damage and can potentially put your opponent to sleep.

Once back in the cells, we'll have to make some decisions. If you'd like, you can free Goemon in the cell on the right using the Dungeon Key we found earlier. After freeing him, you can kill or spare him. It's best to spare him, as Goemon eventually deactivate all the traps in the area and adds some new goodies for you to grab from chests, but it's up to you.

Once you've dealt with him, it's time to make a choice. The samurai we were sent to free is in the cell on the left. Once he's freed, he'll join our cause and become a party member. However, entering the cell to save him commits us to the lethal path. If you want to play non-lethally, leave him for now (he'll join later on his own accord). Otherwise, use the Dungeon Key to enter and walk onto the false floor in front of him.

Freeing The Prisoner

After walking on the panel, you'll be sent cascading into a cave of spirits below. Defeat every spirit in this area. Not only will we need the experience for a fight coming up but these spirits can also heal a tough enemy if they aren't dealt with first, so make sure to take out every single one before progressing. They're weak to water, so rely on the Waterspout ability.

Once they're dead, head up the stairs. You'll come face to face with Amakusa Shiro, who you'll need to challenge and defeat to free the prisoner. The battle itself will vary in difficulty depending entirely on how high a level Oboromaru is. If you're around level 7, you should be able to use Phantom Butterflies to melt away Shiro's health with ease. He's resistant to most moves but wind is effective against him.

However, it's worth being aware of his various abilities. He'll be able to hit you with a lightning attack if you're to his right, as well as absorb your health and hit you with a brutal melee attack if you're one tile in front of him. Keep at range and use Phantom Butterflies to pile on the damage.

Once he falls, you'll be able to recruit the prisoner, who will fall into the cell from the ceiling. Simply talk to him to get him to join your party and leave through the exit behind where Shiro once stood. We'll re-enter the corridor of cells we fell down while trying to free the prisoner. You'll exchange words with the prisoner and then you'll regain control.

Exiting the Dungeons

Head up the stairs to the right of Goemon's cell and you'll reach a second floor of cells. There's another guard in this area that we can kill or spare. If you're playing lethally, use the Dungeon Key to release the merchant down the stairs to the right. He'll ask for food. You can give him some but he'll continue to ask for more until you refuse. This will initiate a fight. Kill him and you'll gain the Devil's Abacus gloves.

You can also take down the two men in the cell on the left-hand side, gaining the Lace Ruff accessory as a reward for the battle.

The prisoner in the north cell is also killable, although he'll put up more of a fight, revealing himself to be a ronin when you release him. When you're ready, head for the sliding doors on the left-hand side of the area. You'll make your way out of dungeons and into the Castle Keep.

Castle Keep, Floor 1

Follow the stairs up and into a room with a Minister meditating. If you're playing non-lethally, ignore him. If you're playing lethally, approach him and he'll call his guards. Two shinobis will drop from the ceiling.

Take them down to unlock the chest in the top right-hand corner, which contains a Kotetsu sword. If you'd like, you can also take down the Minister before leaving. He'll be joined by four candle sticks but they'll fall when he dies, so take him down to end the battle.

Now, head through the southern door opposite the entrance to the area and you'll enter a small passage with a doorway to the south. Instead of heading through the doorway, look for a hidden passage on the right side of the room. It's indicated by two small beams of light on the floor. Use the passage and you'll access a new area with a maid and a chest. Spare the maid for now (she'll run from you regardless) and open the chest to find a scroll.

Head back through the secret passage and, when back in the corridor, head through the southern door. Follow the path until you reach a long balcony overlooking the first floor of the keep.

Four Retainers will be stood here. We can take them out or attempt to evade them. As for where to go when evading the enemies, there's only one door here we need to use right now.

First things first, don't worry about the southern door in the centre of the balcony. That leads to the keep's entrance, and we aren't leaving just yet. As for the door down the stairs on the far-right-hand side, it just leads to a praying maid, and we'll spare her for now regardless of our playstyle.

That leaves only one route: the sliding door next to the top of the staircase on the east side of the area. Head through it and follow the path until you come across three more sliding doors. The door in the centre leads to a minister and two maids. Spare the maids and kill the minister if you wish.

As for the door on the left, it's guarded by a ronin, so give him the password if you're playing non-lethally or slay him if you're playing lethally. Inside, you'll find two chests. One will contain a Shinobi Birdlime and the other a koban.

The door on the right will lead to an elderly man, who will flee out of the left side of the room when you enter.

Don't hit the metal panel in the centre of the room, or wooden stumps will fall from the ceiling and you'll be forced to engage in a combat encounter with the man.

If you do find yourself in the scenario, use Firefall to burn the wood surrounding you and take down the man to pass the encounter.

Whether you fought him or not, Exit through the doors on the left and follow the stairs to Castle Keep's second floor.

Castle Keep, Floor 2

When reaching the second floor, enter the doorway opposite the top of the stairs. Inside, you'll find a maid praying. Leave her be, but loot the pots, chest and sword on the wall before heading back through the entrance.

Take the southern doors and follow the long passage ahead. You'll see a secret passage on your left as you progress down the corridor, but it just leads to some enemies in a crawlspace which you can opt to take down if you need to farm experience. Assuming you aren't interested in stopping to level up, continue down the corridor until you eventually emerge in a large area with a bridge in the centre. There's a circular door across at the end of the bridge that we can investigate.

Enter the circular door and you'll find yourself in a small room with a woman with a cat-like shadow seated in the centre. Much like the character we met in the storeroom earlier, she'll transform into a monster, prompting a new fight. Remember that, as a monster, this woman doesn't count towards our kill number, so non-lethal players can take her down too if they need some extra XP. She can be a difficult battle though, so backtrack to the attic we found earlier if you need to level up.

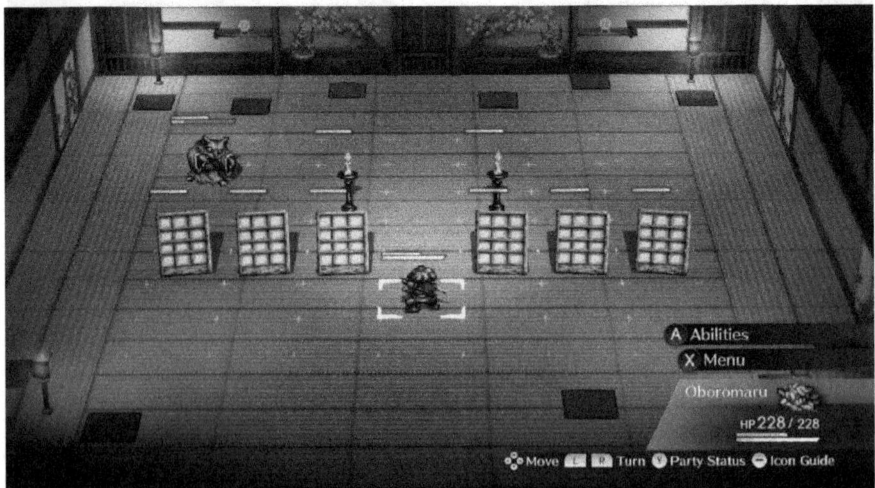

When you spawn into the battlefield, you'll see a row of dividers running through the central line of tiles, as well as two candle sticks and the monster. We only have to take down the monster to succeed, so focus all your attacks on her. As with most enemies at this point of the chapter, it's best to keep your distance and rely on Oboromaru's ranged attacks. If you have The Prisoner, use him to distract the monster, getting in close and dealing melee damage while Oboromaru charges his elemental ranged abilities.

If you have it, Phantom Butterflies works well here, as you can position yourself behind some of the dividers and cast it diagonally at the monster, inflicting a lot of damage. However, the rest of Oboromaru's AOE attacks and ranged moves will do the trick. Keep your distance to grab yourself an easy win.

When she's dead, leave the room, head back across the bridge and make your way to the east side of the area. One Retainer will be patrolling nearby, so dispatch him if you'd like or avoid him. On this side of the room, we'll find two sets of sliding doors. The one on the left leads to three chests that we can't open due to a trap (Goemon will disarm this trap later in the level if we freed him).

The one on the right is guarded by a Retainer, and leads to the third floor. Let's head that way for now. Walk up to the retainer, give him the password if you're playing non-lethally or give him the wrong password and kill him if you're playing lethally. Once you're done, head through the doors and up the stairs ahead to reach the third floor.

Castle Keep, Floor 3

Continue following the path until you reach a room with a ronin and a chest. Kill the ronin if you'd like or spare him.

Either way, make sure to open the chest in the middle of the room to gain the Hook and Rope item. Then, head through the southern door.

Follow the path until you enter a room with a maid inside. A cutscene will trigger where she notices Oboromaru and screams for help. Four shinobis will enter, approaching Oboromaru before they're disrupted by a masked samurai that will challenge them.

His name is Hannyu Maru and he's very, very determined to become an Oni (hey, we all have to have dreams man...). If you're playing non-lethally, avoid him. Otherwise, take down all four enemies and you'll get to fight him yourself.

It's very important that you fight all four shinobis before talking with him if you want to get the maximum number of kills. Every time you attempt to talk to him, he'll kill a nearby shinobi, meaning they don't factor into Oboromaru's kill count.

Despite the build-up, Maru isn't a particularly strong opponent, especially if you've taken down the vast majority of the foes you've encountered up to this point. He fights like the vast majority of the shinobis we found thus far, meaning we'll fall back on the tactics we've honed to get to this point. Focus on using abilities at range and he'll fall quickly.

The more difficult enemy can actually be found north of Maru. If you're opting for a lethal playthrough, head through the sliding doors behind him to enter a room with a praying monk. Talk to him and he'll unleash a tiger hiding in the folding screen behind him.

The ensuing fight is rough at lower levels, but definitely achievable. The trick is to distance yourself from the tiger and keep close enough to the monk to do range damage. However, remember to keep at least two tiles away from the monk at all times. The monk has a ranged ability that can knock off about half of your health if you aren't careful, so playing it safe is the key.

As always, Phantom Butterflies is your best friend here. If you have the Prisoner as well, the fight will be a lot easier, allowing you to use him as a decoy while you unleash powerful spells. Put distance between yourself and the monk, stay at range and you'll carve off chunks of his health bar in no time.

Once you're done with the monk (or if you've skipped the room to remain non-lethal), head east. You'll find a short corridor with two doors and a staircase in the centre. The room on the left will lead to another minister, who will judge you based on how many lives you've taken. If you've taken zero, he'll offer you a reward. Otherwise, he'll ask if you intend to strike him down. Make a choice and leave.

Head through the door to the right of the staircase and you'll find two chests inside. Loot them to find an Enma Charm and scroll.

Castle Keep, Floor 4

Leave the room and head up the staircase in the centre. You'll enter a hallway with two doorways. If we're playing lethally, let's take the door on the right first, following the path through two more corridors and down a flight of stairs.

We'll wind up on a landing with a door and a shinobi. Take down the shinobi or leave him if you're feeling generous. Inside, a cutscene will play, showing a princess being approached by four shinobis. Once it's over and if you're willing to kill all four foes, enter the room and approach the warriors. This fight is tough but all a case of smart positioning.

Head into the top right-hand corner, lure them to your position and use a ranged ability to pick them off. Be careful of the group's shuriken ability, which will slice off half your health bar if it connects.

Once they're done, you'll be able to chat with the maid inside, who will ask if you want to marry her. This princess secretly isn't what she seems, so don't accept. If you do, you'll instantly die, sending you back to your last checkpoint.

Continue talking to the princess until she asks you to marry her once again. Refuse, and you'll be able to kill her. Don't worry, this won't affect the 'no women killed' stat we need to get maximum kills in the mission. With her dead, don't go through the north door, but instead head back to the corridor with two doors we accessed when first reaching the fourth floor. We can technically reach the end of the level from here, but there's more experience to grind through the second route.

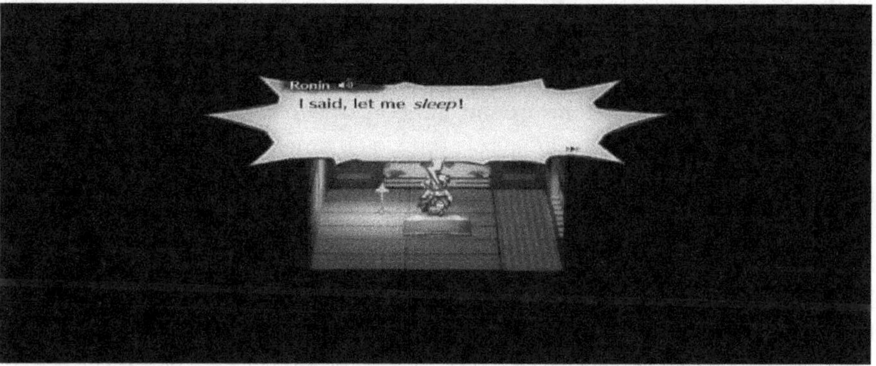

Once you're back at the crossroads, take the left path. You'll enter a long corridor. If you're playing lethally, enter the door in the centre of the path ahead. You'll find a sleeping ronin. Keep talking to him to initiate a battle. This guy will rely on two hard-hitting moves to survive. One is a ranged attack that will hit you if you stand to his right and the other is a melee attack he can execute up close. Use Phantom Butterflies or an equally powerful ranged attack and stay below or diagonal to the ronin. Pick him apart until he falls.

Once he's dead, return to the corridor. There's a secret passage leading to the attic on our left here, so let's take it. Find the fake wall, use it and then follow the path north. Head through a second fake wall and climb the ladder to your right. You'll enter the fourth-floor crawlspace.

Head east here and walk into the nearby group of monsters. You'll initiate a battle (don't worry, this won't count towards your kills, so non-lethal players can slice away). The true objective here is to find and take down the trapper at the top left-hand corner of the screen. Navigate to the left of the pack of monsters and use a ranged attack to target the trapper. Once he's down, the battle will end. Be careful with the monsters, as they can explode (dealing significant damage) if attacked.

Once they're down, continue east into the second gang of monsters. The technique here is similar to the first battle, except the monsters will surround Oboromaru. If you have Wind Slash, use it to attack the trapper from inside the square of monsters. That should finish him off. Otherwise, your best plan is to break out of the square using a powerful AOE attack, giving you the opportunity to circle around to the trapper. Once he's dead, we'll return to the attic.

Continue to your right and loop around. You'll encounter a group of statues you can battle. For the first set (which are blue), you'll only need to defeat the grey statue. He's weak to physical attacks, so use those to bring it down. Once it's finished, continue south and you'll encounter four red statues. You'll have to defeat all four statues this time around, although the method is the same. Physical attacks will finish the lumps of stone in no time at all.

Once you regain control, head down the ladder to your right. At the bottom of the stairs, you'll find a sliding door to your left. Enter it and push onwards to find a small room with a kettle and mug on the table. We're about to take on a tough boss, so switch up your equipment if need be. When you're ready, examine the hidden door at the back of the room. A voice will talk to you from the other side.

The voice will tell you to drink some tea, but don't do it. Instead, keep examining the door. Eventually, it'll ask you whether you trust it. Claim you don't and you'll initiate a battle. Time for our first boss of the area: The Puppetmaster Gennai.

Puppetmaster Gennai Boss Fight

Once we spawn in, we'll find ourselves faced with six enemies and the Puppetmaster Gennai in the corner. Let's quickly get rid of the Puppetmaster's minions, as they'll constantly attack us with electricity while we're trying to end the Puppetmaster. If you have Phantom Butterflies then that's a good way to rid of them fast, however, any other AOE spell should do the job.

Once they're done, attack the Puppetmaster from afar. He'll wield a much stronger electric attack than his small minions, but if you're staying away from his diagonal strikes, you should be able to dodge the majority of them and lay in the damage. Most wind strikes will do the trick, but Shuriken Barrage is also a solid ranged ability that will carve the Puppetmaster's health bar.

If you have the Prisoner, use him as a decoy here, distracting the Puppetmaster while you charge your spells or heal. It shouldn't take long to finish the Puppetmaster, although you can retreat and fight more enemies in the crawlspace if you aren't dealing enough damage.

When he falls, you'll grab the Mainspring key, which we'll need in just a second. Proceed through the fake door north of the tea set.

Optional: Recruiting The Mimic

For this next section, it's crucial we have four Kobans. If you don't, head back through the keep and look for additional chests and loot containing cash. If you freed Goemon, he'll have replenished a few chests, so don't be afraid to return to already scouted areas.

In the room ahead, insert three Kobans into the small black slot in the top-right-hand corner of the room. You'll hear something click. Now, avoid the black tile in the centre of this room (it activates a trap door) and head back through the door to the tea room south of you.

Inside we'll find a small seated figure. Stand to his right-hand side and insert the Mainspring key. It'll power the small figure up, spawning a mimic of Oboromaru (Elden Ring eat your heart out). Defeat the mimic. He shouldn't take too much effort to finish, mostly relying on close-range melee attacks that we can evade using ranged abilities.

Once he's dead, the mimic will join the party, offering you back up in battles. Once you regain control, be very careful not to stand on the button in the centre of the room. It'll cause Oboromaru and the mimic to fall through the floor, breaking the mimic and rendering him useless for the rest of the mission. Exit through the north door and put a final Koban in the slot in the next room. That will reset everything to normal. Once the coin is inserted, enter the sliding door to your left.

With the mimic on our side, it's time to go back for everything we want to do in the level before wrapping things up. If we continue on this path, we'll finish the level (and lose the mimic along the way). While we have the mimic, let's try and take down a few secret bosses. If you just want to take the fastest path to the chapter's conclusion, skip to the next section of the guide.

Optional: Secret Bosses And Farming Experience

Regardless of whether you've slaughtered a host of enemies in this area or not, we're almost certainly going to have to grind up some levels to take on both the secret bosses in this area. There are several ways you can do this, whether that's searching the various attic areas on each level of the keep or hunting down any powerful wandering shinobis you haven't encountered yet.

But the smartest way to quickly boost your level is to head to the Spirit Storehouse. We visited it earlier when using the Storeroom Key, but in case you missed that part, you can find it down the path to the right after exiting through the back door of the Residential Palace. Inside you'll find four spirits that will respawn every time you exit and re-enter the room. They give you a good amount of experience and are incredibly weak, making them essential for farming levels. Head in here and kill these enemies repeatedly until Oboromaru is about level 16.

If you want the fights to be less taxing, you can even boost yourself a little higher, but it's up to you.

Optional: Bloodthirsty Samurai Fight

When you're ready for your first optional fight, head to the Path of Shuttered Lanterns via the wall leading from the Residential Palace attic. If you remember from earlier, to access the mystical corridor we had to leap down from a small wooden outcrop near the room where we found the Storehouse Key. Whatever you do, don't access the shuttered lantern path via the moat. The mimic will break in the water, dying permanently.

Once you're inside the second section of the tunnel, run south. You'll hear a click after a few steps.

Keep moving south until you hear a second click. Don't take another step south. Instead, head back north and use the hidden wall we entered through. When inside, you'll find yourself in a room with a sword on the wall.

Try to grab the sword and a demon will stop you, claiming you have to beat him to unleash its power. To be frank, the boss fight ahead is brutal, so make sure you save and get ready to retry a few times. Regardless, here's the strategy for taking this bloodthirsty samurai down:

When you load into the level, the demon samurai will be in the top left corner. The easiest way to approach this battle is to stick Oboromaru in the bottom right-hand corner where he can execute ranged attacks with heavy damage while the Mimic and the Prisoner (if you have them) distract the samurai.

Use a combination of Winter's Chill, Wind Slash, Phantom Butterflies and Phoenix Call to do damage. Whatever you do, do not stand to the samurai's right or left. He has a brutal spell that will near enough one-shot you if you fall into its range. Meanwhile, use the Prisoner and the Mimic to draw the samurai's attention, using physical attacks or spells to deal small damage that pulls his attention away.

Most of the samurai's attacks are diagonal, with him lining up an opponent two tiles away and laying into them. That means the Mimic and the Prisoner should get in close to avoid being knocked down quickly.

It's very likely that the samurai will make short work of both of your companions and come directly for Oboromaru, at which point we need to end the fight fast. There are a few options here. We can make a desperate ploy to reposition Oboromaru, using Demented Spin to ensure he's facing away and give us time to shuffle to another corner of the battlefield before he can strike you down with his electric attack. Or, we can also use Dustveil to attempt to bind him.

If you do manage to bind him you can either run for the opposite corner and try to finish him off with ranged attacks or, if you're feeling daring, make a bold play, standing directly to the samurai's right or left and executing Deepest Dark (a Slash Attack gained at level 14 that can one-shot an opponent if you're lucky). If you're successful, the attack can instantly kill the samurai, getting you an easy win.

Deepest Dark should be your last resort, because the samurai will be able to one-shot you with his electric attack if you fail. Play it smart and safe unless there's no other way to avoid his moves.

I won't sugarcoat it. This fight sucks, so don't get disheartened if he keeps beating you to a pulp. If things are too tough, return to the storeroom, beat up some spirits, level up and return. Once you take him down, you'll get the Muramasa, which is a sword that deals massive damage. You can equip it after grabbing it from the wall at the back of the room.

Optional: Lord Iwama Secret Boss Fight

Before we slay our second boss, we'll first want to get rid of the Mimic (if we have him). Although he can survive until we reach Lord Iwama, the likelihood is that he'll die shortly after we enter the moat as water kills him permanently.

If you're playing fully lethally, don't worry about the next step. It'll wind up killing three enemies, meaning we can't reach the 100 kill count. Just let the Mimic die in the moat. For non-lethal players or those not concerned about kill count, Return all the way back to the tea room, head through the fake wall, enter the door at the back of the next room and go through the exit on your left. Follow the route until you enter a room with three guards.

The Mimic will go haywire in this room after seeing a mouse, exploding and killing all three guards. When they're dead, the Mimic can be found broken on the floor (rest in peace, king). If the Mimic is going to die in the moat, he might as well go down in a blaze of glory and save us fighting three more enemies instead of simply sinking into the abyss.

Now, return to the moat. You can access it via the Path of Shuttered Lanterns or the bottom of the Keep's Dungeons. On the second level of the moat, you'll find a large black mass swimming around. Run into it and we'll access our second secret boss fight in this area: Lord Iwama... I think the name kind of undersells that the dude's literally just a GIANT fish.

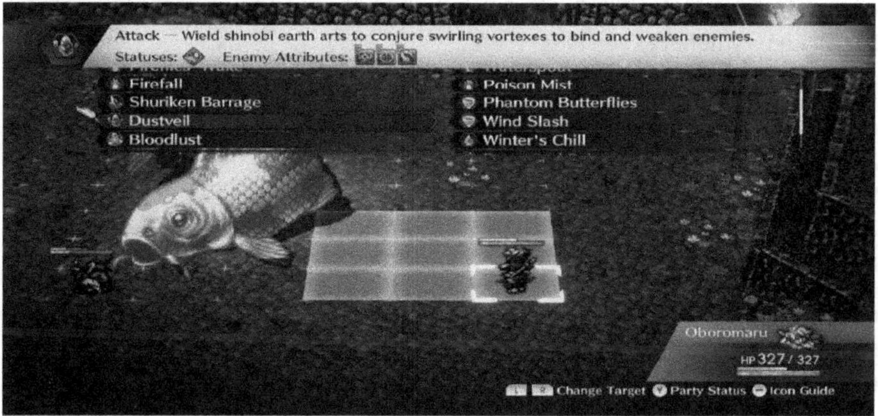

Anyway, time to catch us some koi. Assuming we have the Prisoner by now, the strategy is to put Oboromaru in the bottom right-hand corner of the screen and the prisoner in the bottom left-hand corner. The worst thing about Lord Iwama is his size. There's no real point running from the large fish as he doesn't have to move around the arena much to catch you. With this placement, we'll force him to move between both party members while keeping them close enough to give each other revives.

There are really only three moves we're watching out for here. If you're standing one tile in front of the fish, he'll be able to use a trample move to inflict huge damage and knock you back. This is inevitably going to hit you a few times throughout the fight, so it's best to learn when to tank this to get a hit in and when to back off. He also has a weaker melee attack that can be executed from a diagonal position. This is the best of the three moves to be hit with, and shouldn't do too much damage unless the big fish gets lucky.

Finally, there's his wave move, which is the real killer here. The initial attack won't do much damage, but the water tiles it leaves will heal Lord Iwama. This means a useful trick to beating him is wiping these tiles off the map and replacing them with different elemental tiles as fast as you can. Using Fireflies' Wake is an easy way to do this (and will turn the tides on Iwama, as fire tiles will heal Oboromaru), although Lord Iwama is so big that he will still likely absorb water tiles no matter what you do.

With these attacks in mind, a solid strategy is to use Warning Shot (if you have the Prisoner in your party) and Dustveil to lock Lord Iwama in place with bind. From here, it's all about using physical attacks to knock down his health, laying down fire tiles with Fireflies' Wake when he lays down water tiles and spamming health items whenever you need them.

In terms of dealing damage, you have a few good moves to rely on. Dustveil will deal decent damage and has a chance of interrupting Iwama's attacks (as well as binding him). Meanwhile, Shuriken Barrage hits hard and Deepest Dark will knock his health bar down fast or potentially one-shot him if you're lucky (at the expense of needing to get up in Iwama's face). Remain patient and keep healing. Iwama should eventually go down.

Once he does, you'll gain the Sujin Scale accessory, which dramatically boosts Special Attack power. Equip it and return to the room with the three guards the Mimic blew up earlier. It's time to finish this.

Miyamoto Musashi Battle

Once you're back in the room where the Mimic died earlier, push through the sliding door in the centre. You'll find eight shinobi and Lord Ode. Walk into the middle of the room and these warriors will challenge you to a fight. If you didn't rescue the Prisoner, he'll arrive here and take the eight warriors down, maintaining your non-lethal streak and having him join the party. However, if you did rescue him, then we'll have to fight them all.

This seems like an intimidating scenario, although it's actually quite easy if you're high enough level. If you have Phoenix Call, select it and make sure all the shinobi are lined up in the radius. Choose it and you'll eviscerate them all in no time.

Once they're dead, Ode will flee, leaving you to fight the spirit of Miyamoto Musashi. This will lead us to a boss fight.

Musashi is much more of a pushover than the two secret bosses we just clashed swords with, although the technique mostly remains the same. Send Oboromaru to the bottom right-hand corner and use the Prisoner to play decoy.

Although Musashi is resistant to spells, don't be afraid to use them as they'll still do a lot of damage. In particular, Winter's Chill, Phantom Butterflies and Wind Slash will all hurt Musashi despite his resistance to the elements. Use the Prisoner's abilities to distract Musashi, stunning him with Warning Shot if you can.

The combo of both Oboromaru's ranged abilities and Musashi's physical attacks should get the job done quickly, especially if you farmed experience to beat the two secret bosses found earlier in the mission.

Demon Battle

With Musashi down, head through the door at the back right-hand side of the room. Continue down the path until you reach a staircase. The woman who potentially offered to marry us earlier will appear (if you're a non-lethal player and didn't visit that room, listen, it's a long story...). After a short conversation with her, she'll transform into a demon and we'll be forced to fight.

The strategy here is the same as always. Send Oboromaru to the bottom right-hand corner and use the Prisoner as a distraction. Ice is particularly effective against this demon, so rely on Winter's Chill to do damage.

As for the demon, she'll rely on a spinning attack which she can execute against anyone 3 tiles in front of her. It doesn't hit too hard though, especially if you've farmed to reach a higher level.

Once she's down, we'll push on ahead. In the next room, if we haven't killed a single woman in the run-through so far, we'll be interrupted by a maid when attempting to enter the sliding door. She'll give us a gift (the Maid's Sash).

If we wait for a few seconds, she'll come back, giving us her true gift: the Lacquered Medicine Box accessory. If you refuse the gifts, you can kill her. She's the secret NPC I referenced needing to find to reach 100 kills earlier.

If you did kill her and are aiming to reach the 100 kill maximum, you can now head back through the keep and kill every female NPC you've seen so far. If you've been vigilant and taken down every NPC, that should raise your kill count to the max. Great job! You're a cold-blooded murderer!

If you're playing non-lethally or don't care about kill count, let's push on.

Point of No Return Warning

This next battle will officially end our time with Oboromaru and the Prisoner. You know what that means.

Time to add all the best equipment to Oboro's inventory. Any quipment left on The Prisoner won't come with Oboromaru when he takes on the final chapter, so ensure everything's put on the shinobi by the time Lord Ode's in our sights.

Lord Ode Battle

When you're prepped, head through the north door. It's time to take down Ode once and for all. Inside the room ahead, Ode will be sat meditating.

After Oboromaru and the Prisoner enter, Ode will taunt them and we'll start the fight. This is actually only the first phase of Ode's battle, and by extension, it shouldn't take too long to best him.

Ode has a pistol and can fire it at any opponent diagonal to him. He also has a poison attack that he can offload onto any enemy a tile in front of him. Neither inflicts huge damage, so don't worry about tanking them while you hit him.

Elemental attacks are really going to make the difference here, so back Oboromaru up and use Winter's Chill, Wind Slash, Phantom Butterflies, Phoenix Call or any other powerful ranged elemental strike you have in your arsenal.

Ode should go down quickly. Once he does, he'll tell you to meet him on the roof, and flee. Head back into the corridor where we met the maid and through the door south of you. A cutscene will then play, as Ode transforms himself into a giant frog monster... because of course he does...

It's time for phase 2. You know the drill now. Position Oboromaru in the bottom right-hand corner and have the Prisoner get up close and personal. Frog Ode is weak to Bloodlust and Warning Shot, and doesn't have any elemental weaknesses, so lay into him with Wind Slash, Phantom Butterflies, Winter's Chill or any other long-ranged spell.

As for his attacks, he can melee attack and absorb health from any foe one tile away from him. Neither do massive damage, so stay away from him and it shouldn't take long to whittle away his health, especially if you've spent time levelling Oboromaru and the Prisoner up to take down the secret bosses.

Once he's dead, the Prisoner will reveal his name is Sakamoto Ryoma. He'll offer Oboromaru to join his cause. We'll get the option to accept or turn down this offer. Make your choice and the chapter will conclude.

The Wild West

Featuring tense duels, booby traps and an enemies-turned-allies storyline, Live A Live's Wild West chapter is one of its more story-focused attractions. While an epic gunfight is at the centre of the tale, a lot of the build-up to that battle sees us talking with locals, preparing traps and learning more about our mysterious protagonist: Sundown.

The walkthrough below will give you all the tips and tricks needed to complete the chapter, including how to build all the traps, win every battle and even secure a secret conclusion.

Looking for a specific section of the chapter? Jump between sections using the link below:

The Wild West

The Wild West chapter opens with a sheriff entering a desolate saloon. After some brief banter with the bartender, he'll ask him to hang a wanted poster on the wall. The bartender will oblige, looking for the name of the bounty while hanging it on the wall.

Turns out that's our cue to name the main protagonist of this chapter. The default name for this wandering gunslinger is Sundown (and that's what we'll be referring to him as throughout the chapter), although you're free to call him whatever you like.

After naming our mysterious protagonist, we'll cut to him riding through the desert. After a short scene, his journey is interrupted as he runs into a bounty hunter by the name of Mad Dog, who challenges Sundown to a duel.

We'll cut to the battlefield, giving us our first taste of Live A Live's Wild West throwdowns. Position Sundown so he's diagonal to Mad Dog and use Hollow Point to knock him backwards. He'll likely hit you on his turn, but it'll cause Sundown to use the Quickdraw ability as a counterattack. Fire at Mad Dog again to finish the fight.

Once it's done, Sundown will spare Mad Dog and ride away, leaving him stranded in the desert. After a short ride, he'll arrive at the town we saw at the beginning of the chapter.

A Small Town Called Success

Following a title screen, we'll see Sundown ride through a town called Success on his horse. It's the same locale we saw briefly during the opening of the chapter. Once you regain control, make your way to the Crystal Saloon. It's on the west side of the town, marked by the golden flag on your mini-map.

Enter the saloon. The locals inside will quiet down immediately, taking a seat. None of them will talk to Sundown if you attempt to chat, so just head over to the bar. Before you talk to the bartender, head around the bar and open the pot to his left. It'll contain a Herbal Liniment.

Circle back around the bar and chat to the bartender. He'll ask if Sundown wants to order anything, triggering a series of events where an outlaw enters the saloon and causes havoc. The outlaw will attempt to intimidate Sundown, asking him to move seats before a barmaid comes downstairs and shouts at him.

After a heated exchange, she'll slap him. Before he can retaliate, the Sheriff's son runs in and the outlaw throws him into Sundown, causing him to turn his attention back to the mysterious gunslinger. After a short discussion, he'll buy you a glass of milk. You can drink or refuse it; it doesn't matter which option you pick. He'll then joke that Sundown would only like the milk if it was his mother's, to which we can pick one of two responses: stay quiet or say "your mother's, maybe".

We'll eventually get into a fight with this man regardless of what we say. Move diagonal of the Outlaw and use Hollow Shot. It'll finish him in one hit, ending the fight instantly.

When we return to the scene, the outlaw will run away, declaring that his battle with Sundown is far from over.

Once he's gone, the townspeople will ask Sundown to help them deal with a gang of outlaws bothering the town. The sheriff will then arrive. As they attempt to tell him what happened, their excitement is cut short when Mad Dog appears, revealing Sundown's true identity.

The Sheriff's son Billy will run to Sundown, asking him whether he's a good guy. There are two options here, but we have to choose "I'm no Saint" to keep the scene moving.

Mad Dog will challenge us to a duel, leaving the saloon and telling Sundown to meet him outside. After he's gone, you'll regain control. Save the game and head outside when you're ready.

When you leave, we'll see Sundown and Mad Dog preparing to duel. Just as they're about to shoot, they both turn and gun down two outlaws sneaking up on them.

After a chat with the townsfolk, the pair agree to team up for the time being to help the community deal with the outlaws.

Preparing Traps for Dawn

We'll then cut to a scene in the saloon at night. Once you regain control, chat to the townsfolk nearby. They'll reveal some minor details, the most important being the name of the leader of the outlaws' leader: O.Dio. When you're ready to move on, chat to Mad Dog. He's sat at a table at the bottom right-hand corner of the screen. He'll tell Sundown they need to prepare traps to ambush the outlaws.

Mad Dog calls on the aid of the townsfolk to help booby trap the town, with everyone agreeing to help. Once the scene concludes, the main part of this chapter will officially begin.

We'll need to prepare for a showdown taking place the following morning, finding items and using them to plant traps around the town. The catch is that we can't take our time planning. We'll have until the eighth bell to prepare, which is around 15 minutes.

In that time, we'll have to search each building in town, raiding chests, drawers and pots to scrounge together supplies. You'll know which buildings you've searched if they're marked blue on the mini-map. Once we have the supplies, we'll have to sacrifice time to build traps, sending the townsfolk away on errands and hoping they return before the eighth bell sounds.

As for the time, it'll tick away as we go. You can see how long you have left via the bell meter in the top right-hand corner of the screen. Mad Dog will also note whenever a bell rings, counting you down. If you want to move the scene on, talk to the Sheriff. He'll begin the trap planning phase.

The more traps we place, the fewer enemies we'll eventually have to face off against. If you're dead set on taking on all of the Crazy Bunch without traps, you can, but you're going to have a rough go of it.

So, let's run through the best scenario you can earn from preparing a successful ambush. We'll run through all the buildings in the town of Success and what you can find in each.

Crystal Saloon: 7 Items

Once you regain control, save your game immediately. If things go pear-shaped, we'll have to reload back to this point and try again. Head up to the bar's second floor and enter the room on the far left. You'll find a Strip of Jerky in a chest in the back of the room.

Next, head to the room on the far right. In the locker at the back of the room, you'll find the Bartender's Special Poster. When you've got the poster, head downstairs and enter the door in the back right-hand corner. You'll find a Miracle Tonic, a Herbal Liniment and some Oil inside. With that room empty, leave and head through the door to the left of the bar. Head to the chest to the right of the desk to find another Herbal Liniment.

With all those resources grabbed, leave through the front door and head into the building opposite the saloon.

Diner: 3 Items

You'll enter the diner. Head behind the counter on the left side of the room and open the barrel to find some Oil. Now, head through the door directly south of the oil barrel. You'll enter a backroom.

Loot the Frying Pan accessory off the wall and then open the barrel in the corner to find a Carrot. With both of these in your inventory, head through the front door and back onto the street. This time, enter the building to the right of the Crystal Saloon.

Post Office: 3 Items

You'll find yourself in the town's Post Office. Look for a door beneath the stairs and head through it. You'll enter a backroom. Loot the chest in front of you to find another Strip of Jerky. Follow the path around and you'll find a second door leading behind the desk we saw when entering the post office.

There should be a chest to your right. Loot it to find the Empty Bottle. Assuming you visited the Diner first and got the Oil, Mad Dog will offer to combine them, noting it'll take some time. Agree and he'll fashion a Bottled Fire projectile. Every time Mad Dog offers this, accept.

Now, return to the entrance to the post office and head up the stairs we saw earlier. Ignore the door north of you and instead enter the south door. Loot the chest directly next to the door you entered through to find a Herbal Liniment. With all those items grabbed, leave through the Post Office's front door and head to the barn opposite you.

Larder: 1 Item

Not much to see here. Examine the cart to the right of the door. You'll find a Shovel. Grab it and then head back outside.

We'll now head to the Sheriff's Office, which is to the right of the Post Office. This one's easier to spot thanks to the sign above the door. Head inside.

Sheriff's Office: 4 Items

When you enter the Sheriff's Office, you'll see a desk in front of you and a staircase to your left. Loot the chests behind the desk to find a Peacemaker and a stick of Dynamite, then loot the desk to find a Strip of Jerky.

When you've grabbed all three items, ascend the staircase and head into the room upstairs. There's nothing in the chest to your left, but the compartment below the window next to the chest contains a Buntline Special.

With all the items found, leave the Sheriff's Office and head to the lodge opposite you. This is the Miner's Lodge.

Miner's Lodge: 1 Item

There's only one item in the Miner's Lodge and it's found in the back room. Head to the door southeast of the entrance. Inside, you'll discover a chest to your right. Open it to find an Empty Bottle.

With that grabbed, exit the lodge and head all the way back to Crystal Saloon. We're now going to scrounge through the resources on the west side of town. Head into the barn to the left of the Crystal Saloon.

Brewery: 1 Item

Inside, we'll find the Brewery. There's only one item in here. Head to the back right-hand corner of the room to find a Miracle Tonic. Add that to your inventory. Now, head back out through the entrance.

Once outside, head for the building opposite the brewery. Inside, you'll find Wayne's Boarding House.

Wayne's Boarding House: 1 Item

While the boarding house is big and has an overwhelming number of rooms, it's actually just a giant red herring. There's only one item of use here, and it's pretty tricky to spot. From the entrance, head left and follow the route through a door to a back room.

Here, you'll see a large staircase leading up to a landing with three doors. Ignore the second floor completely, and walk across the first floor until you're aligned with the middle of the staircase, in front of the three barrels circled above. It's hard to spot, but there's actually a door here. Move Sundown up and, if you're in the right spot, he'll enter the room.

Loot the chest in the back left-hand corner to find a Bundle of Rope. Now, leave the Boarding House and head inside the building to the left of the Brewery. This is the Sheriff's House.

Sheriff's House: 1 Item

The only room we need to go into here is below the stairs. Head inside and look in the pot in the centre of the room. You'll find some Oil.

Now, leave the Sheriff's House and head to the barn southwest of the Sheriff's House.

Stables: 3 Items

Once inside, head to the pile of hay opposite you and interact with it. You'll find some Horse Dung. Now, loot the chest to the right of the hay pile. You'll find a Carrot. Finally, head upstairs and loot the chest to find another Empty Bottle.

With all three items grabbed, leave the stables and head to the building opposite. You'll enter the Storehouse.

Storehouse: 3 Items

In the two chests in the back left-hand corner of the room, you'll find two Carrots. Meanwhile, in the chest to your right when entering, you'll find some Coal Tar.

With all three items, leave the Storehouse and return to the Crystal Saloon. It's time to set our plan into motion.

Distributing Supplies

Talk to the sheriff when you've found everything you need for the showdown. After a short discussion, he'll recommend distributing the supplies between the group. There are only two traps that are character-specific, and the only one we currently have is the Frying Pan, which we can give to Annie. Before you willingly donate it though, it's worth noting that you can keep the frying pan and use it to boost your defence by equipping it as an accessory. How you use it is up to you but I'd recommend keeping it.

When designating traps, the sheriff will warn you that some characters are slower than others at setting traps, which is something you'll want to keep in mind.

When speaking to each character, they'll give you an idea of how reliable they are, which clues us into how fast they are at setting traps. If you were quick during the item section, you should be making good time anyway, so we don't have to worry too much about the townsfolk's speeds.

When asked to assign trap-building duties, these are the characters you should rely on most:

Annie

The Sheriff

The Barman

James

Dallas

Wayne

Give them traps like the Rope, Shovel, Coal Tar, Horse Manure, Barman's Poster and Frying Pan (if you aren't keeping it). Then delegate out one Bottled Fire, Dynamite and Carrot to Sancho, Pancho or Cesar. Only give them one of these items, as using multiple won't lead to any additional deaths. Finally, head up to Billy and talk to him. He'll give you the Slingshot. Immediately return it, designating him the Slingshot as his trap and we'll be good to go.

After assigning Billy his slingshot, wait for the barman to return if he's still planting a trap and talk to him. Pick "..." and he'll offer to pour you a drink. Accept the drink to end this segment.

We're ready to take down some outlaws. Remember, if things didn't go exactly to plan and your time was off, just reload your previous save and run the scenario again. Once you know the plan inside and out, you'll shave off plenty of time.

Point of No Return

Before we have a drink with the bartender, let's quickly equip Sundown with all the best gear currently equipped on Mad Dog. We'll be able to use it during the Final Chapter unless Mad Dog takes it with him into this final fight.

Final Showdown and O.Dio Boss Battle

If we were successful with our traps, you'll get to watch as the items you gathered decimate the Crazy Bunch, knocking them from their horses, blowing them up and generally causing chaos.

Depending on how many traps you set up, you can essentially wipe out the entire gang but its leader: O.Dio.

After the cutscene concludes, Sundown and Mad Dog will prepare to face this legendary outlaw. You'll get two dialogue options (don't worry, they don't change anything) and then Mad Dog and Sundown will head out to face their foe.

After a short interaction, it's time to take these outlaws out for good. A fight will begin. As O.Dio wields a large mini-gun, we really don't want to fight him at range. Take out any stragglers you didn't manage to finish off with the traps. The standard outlaws are vulnerable to wind attacks, so Hollow Point or Through and Through will make short work of them.

Once they're down, focus on O.Dio. Get right up in his face. He'll have a melee attack called Flaming Cocktail which hits with fire damage, but it won't do much to Sundown or Mad Dog, so it's easy to tank.

His ranged attack, however, isn't as easy to dodge. If you see him charging it, you'll have two options. The first is to move two lanes away from the attack. If you're below him, that means moving two tiles to the right. If you're to his right, that means moving two tiles down and if you're diagonal, that means moving two tiles down or up. If you aren't in the dodging mood though, the more reliable option is to interrupt him while he's charging the strike. As Sundown, use Hollow Point. If you hit, his move will be interrupted, cancelling it out.

Just stay close, hit him with big shots and you should be able to take him down quickly. Once he falls, the town will come outside and celebrate. O.Dio's body will then... uh... turn into a purple horse? Yeah, considering O.Dio is an evil horse spirit determined to gain revenge for the death of his battalion, you would have thought he'd be a more harrowing colour than My-Little-Pony-Purple. Anyway, Mad Dog will then decide it's time to finish things between him and Sundown, challenging you to the duel you were going to have earlier.

This will initiate a battle. Mad Dog will mainly just uses Sidewinder, which hits diagonally. It'll do a lot of damage, but you also hit pretty hard. Pick flee from the menu if you want to spare Mad Dog or repeatedly hit him with Hollow Point if you want to kill him. There isn't a huge repercussion for killing or sparing the bounty hunter, but you will get an additional scene as a reward for sparing him.

After dealing with the bounty hunter, you'll get to see a short interaction between the townspeople and Sundown.

They'll offer him money and he'll refuse, claiming he just wanted to do something decent for a change. And with that, the chapter will come to a close.

Present Day

Arguably Live A Live's most unconventional chapter, Present Day transforms this story-focused RPG into an arcadey fighting game, seeing us pick opponents and fight them in wacky arenas around the globe.

Players take on the role of Masaru Takahara: a formidable fighter hoping to hone his craft by beating the best martial artists in the world.

The walkthrough below will show you how best to spend this short but action-packed chapter, including how to unlock every learnable move.

Looking for a specific fight? Skip between each battle using the links below:

Present Day	Max Morgan Fight	Jackie Laukea Fight	Seishi Moribe Fight
Tula Han Fight	Namkiat Fight	Great Aja Fight	Final Boss Fight

Present Day

The Present Day chapter will open on a cutscene, showing a muscle-bound hero working out and monologuing about his desire to be the greatest fighter in the world. To accomplish his lofty goal, he intends to conquer every martial art and defeat the master practitioners that study them.

After watching his very Rocky 4 workout montage, we'll get the opportunity to name this ambitious underdog. The default name is Masaru Takahara (and for the sake of simplicity, that's the name we'll be using throughout this guide), but feel free to change it to whatever you please.

Following this motivational speech, we'll cut to a fighter select screen. From here we can pick one of six fighters to battle. This boss gauntlet can be tackled in any order, although there are some moves you'll learn from defeating certain fighters that'll help immensely if you get them early.

Before we hop into the boss fights, let's quickly explain how this Present Day chapter works. When you load up a fight, you'll go head to head with your opponent immediately.

When they hit you with one of their signature moves, Takahara will learn it, adding it to his arsenal. If you miss out on a move, don't worry; you can replay any fight after completing it from the Fighter Select screen.

Our goal during each and every bout is to bait out a fighter's best move and then use it against them.

Fight 1: Max Morgan

Let's start our journey with Hulk Hog- I mean Max Morgan. This professional wrestler will go toe to toe with you in a wrestling ring, dressed in stars and stripes spandex and sporting a stunning handlebar moustache. The moves we can learn from him are the Max Bomber and German Suplex.

As soon as the battle starts, run over to Max and perform a Rolling Wheel Kick to spin him around. He'll hit you with a Max Bomber, adding that to our move set. Next, stand in front of Morgan and hit him with a punch. You'll anger him, causing him to go full Brock Lesnar and pull off a German Suplex, adding that to our roster of moves.

The Max Bomber into a German Suplex combo will probably have left you pretty beat up, so let's use Takahara's Focus ability to heal up. This power removes any status ailments and adds health, meaning we can use it whenever we're in a jam. It's best to retreat to a corner to use the ability, as it can leave you defenceless if an enemy is nearby. If Morgan gets close, move to another corner and keep using the move until you're fully healed.

When you're back in fighting shape, use German Suplex on Max Morgan to inflict a ton of damage. Keep moving around the arena, hitting him with German Suplexes and Max Bombers. The German Suplexes might paralyse him, at which point you'll want to follow up with another attack before moving away. If you need to heal, head to a corner ASAP and use Focus.

It shouldn't take long for big Max to fall. When he's down, we'll return to the fighter select screen.

Fight 2: Jackie Laukea

For our second fight, take a look at the combatant on the far right-hand side of the screen. Jackie Laukea is the sumo master, hailed as a once-in-a-generation talent. The description tells us he was once aiming to become a yokozuna, before giving up on the dream to dominate MMA. His abilities are Aloha Clap, Worldbreaker Slam and Mano Toss.

Select him and we'll be transported to a secluded beach. After you regain control, immediately run up to Laukea. Hit him with a Rolling Wheel Kick and he'll react by hitting you with a Mano Toss into a Worldbreaker's Wrath. The combo will give you two of Laukea's moves, although you'll definitely be in bad shape. Retreat to a corner and use Focus to regain your health.

Use it as many times as you need, moving corners if Laukea gets too close. Once you're back at full health, it's time to get back in there for round 2. Run up to Laukea and wait directly in front of him. Eventually, he'll hit you with an Aloha Slap, adding that to your roster of moves.

With all three moves learned, let's take this sumo practitioner down for good. Hit Laukea with a Mano Toss and then charge up a Worldbreaker's Wrath and use it on him. There's a good chance he'll try to snap you out of the move with one of his own, but keep attempting to hit it, as it does massive damage.

Keep using both moves while staying just out of Lakeua's reach. Retreat to a corner if you need to heal with Focus. If you string your moves together smartly then, before you know it, the sumo giant should topple. With him finished, we'll once again return to the Fighter Select screen.

Fight 3: Seishi Moribe

With Lakeua down for the count, let's turn our attention to Seishi Moribe; the elderly man in the centre of the select screen. His description tells us he's a practitioner of Koppo, with the master supposedly knowing a brutal move that can kill a man in one hit. His moves are Fleetfoot and Celestial Palm.

Moribe's encounter takes place in a desolate courtyard. Once you gain control, move towards the old man and wait directly below him. Moribe is weak, and you'll likely defeat him in no time if you charge in there with big attacks. However, we're here to learn his strikes, so don't go in there looking for a scrap. From this position, he'll eventually hit us with Fleetfoot, adding that to our roster.

When you've learnt that, you'll want to hover one tile in front of Moribe to get him to use Celestial Palm. Now, this move can be hell to learn, as Moribe is incredibly stingy with his use of it. Sometimes he'll deploy it four times in a row; other times he won't even use it once.

Hover one tile in front of Moribe until he uses the move, dipping in and out of range to use Focus and heal up when needed. If Takahara counters Moribe with Mano Toss too many times, Moribe may unintentionally die, in which case just reboot his battle from the Fighter Select screen. When he does hit Celestial Palm and add it to your roster, use it to defeat him and we'll move on to our next fight.

Fight 4: Tula Han

Our next battle is the Russian fighter found next to Moribe on the Fighter Select screen: Tula Han. This submission specialist is a former special forces operator, known for dismantling opponents with brutal limb locks. His special moves are the Armlock and the Cross Heel Hold.

The fight will take place in a snowy fighting pit. When you gain control, run up to Han and hit him with a Rolling Wheel Kick. After you land, he'll likely reverse the attack into a Cross Heel Hold, allowing us to add the move to our arsenal.

Attack him again in a one tile radius and he'll use Armlock, adding that to our repertoire. At this point, you'll almost certainly be bound by his moves and there's little point trying to escape the status effect, as all his attacks have a chance of inflicting it. We'll have to finish him in the pocket. If you need health, use Focus. Otherwise, use Worldbreaker Slam to chip away at his health bar. It shouldn't take too long to fell the Russian giant.

Fight 5: Namkiat

For our penultimate fight, let's take on Namkiat. This Muay Thai champion hails from Thailand and is known for his blisteringly fast knockout kicks. Looks like we're going to have to take some of them on the chin to learn his two special moves: Lookpanjama Kick and Spiral Knee.

The battle will take place on a crowded street. When you gain control, rush towards Namkiat and land a Rolling Wheel Kick. Keep landing them until Namkiat counters you with the Lookpanjama Kick. He'll likely combo that with a Spiral Knee the turn after, allowing us to learn both of his key moves at once.

However, if he doesn't, stand one tile away from where he's facing and he should try to land the move. Once both moves are in your arsenal, flee to a corner and use Focus until you're back to full health. Once you are, use the Lookpanjama Kick to keep Namkiat at bay, peppering in the German Suplex and Cross Heel Hold to chip off his health (he's vulnerable to both moves).

If you need to heal, retreat to a corner and use Focus. Before long, Namkiat will be defeated. Bringing us to our final fight.

6th Fight: The Great Aja

And with that, there's only one fighter left: The Great Aja. This Mexican wrestler is known by some as the Angel of Death, mainly due to his love of bending the rules and hurting his opponents. We'll have another two special moves to watch out for here: The Frankensteiner and the Tornado Press.

The fight will take place in another wrestling ring, albeit with much more Luchadore charm than the All-American flair we witnessed when fighting Max Morgan. Get in close with Aja and stand one tile diagonal of him. Remain in the pocket and pass turns until Aja uses the Frankensteiner.

It'll disorientate Takahara but he'll add the move to his arsenal. Here's where things get tricky. Aja rarely uses the Tornado Press, but when he does, it'll likely be when you're two tiles below him. Stay in this area and heal. Eventually, he should bring out Tornado Press, adding it to our arsenal.

To chip off the rest of his health, use either Lookpanjama Kick or Spiral Knee. He's vulnerable to both attacks, making them useful tools to defeat him quickly. Once he's done, we'll be prompted to save the game.

Fight 7: Odie O'Bright

The scene will then cut to Takahara wandering a waterfront. He'll meet a strange man who calls Takahara weak for sparing the lives of his opponents. The stranger will reveal that he's killed all of the combatants we've faced so far, claiming to be the ultimate martial artist.

Takahara calls on the power of every fighter he conquered, summoning all his strength and deciding to face this man, who reveals his name is Odie O'Bright. We'll then enter a battle with Odie.

Don't worry, we aren't learning moves here. Simply bring everything you've learnt to the table and beat this guy to a pulp.

Odie is the largest opponent we'll face in this chapter, and for the most part, that's the toughest thing about him. His main move is known as Reaper's Scythe, which hits Takahara if he's one tile away. So, let's stay at range, using moves like Tornado Press, Spiral Knee, Fleetfoot and Worldbreaker's Wrath to hit Odie. He can use another move known as Bonebreaker (it hits if you're two tiles to his left or below him), but it's a weak move that won't cause much damage.

Eventually, he'll begin charging a far more significant move (you'll know as his wait meter will turn red). Move at least three tiles away from him and three tiles up or down from the lane you were in when the meter started charging. He'll unleash a move known as Diving DDO that deals huge damage if it lands.

Rinse and repeat the cycle, retreating from Odie if you need to heal. Make sure you don't get hit with Diving DDO and you should be able to take him down in no time.

When you do, you'll be treated to a cutscene of Odie's defeat, showing Takahara recovering as a new challenger approaches. Ain't no rest for the wicked, time to start training for Tyson Fury...

The Near Future

Tired of using katanas, clubs and revolvers? Luckily, Live A Live's Near Future chapter is here with massive mechs, robots possessed by the souls of dead turtles and psychic wizardry.

Akira's tale is easily one of the most out there in the entire game and it's also crammed with stuff to do. The walkthrough below will help you navigate through this sci-fi world, showing you how to get the best items through upgrading, acquire the most powerful abilities and sell a LOAD of taiyaki.

Looking for something specific? Jump between sections using the links below:

Near Future

The Near Future chapter opens with a mysterious character asking whether you're satisfied in life. You'll be able to select yes or no. This character will then vow to tell you his story, with the opening cutscene showing him watch his father die at the hands of a biker gang called The Crusaders.

Following the flashback, we'll cut to a scene where he and his sister move into an orphanage. The carer will ask him to introduce himself to the other kids. It's here we'll get to name our character. The default name is Akira (and that's what we're going to call him throughout this walkthrough), but you can select whatever you like.

Akira will tell us that the orphanage made him realise a lot of things, namely that he had strange powers. He could read minds and move things with telekinesis. He even lets us know that he controls his powers by hitting the Y button... very specific that, isn't it? When prompted, hit the Y button and continue the scene.

Welcome to The Future

After the introduction concludes, Akira will wake up on a bench in the centre of a park. Let's quickly get used to the reading minds mechanic.

Walk up to any of the citizens roaming the park and hit Y when directly next to them. A thought bubble will pop up, revealing what the subject is thinking.

Once you're used to the power, head east, proceeding down the path to the right of the nearby food stall. A cutscene will play, with four kids wearing skeleton masks cornering Akira. Once the cutscene ends, read the mind of the kid to Akira's left. It'll reveal he's worried about meeting a "quota", claiming he's going to kidnap Akira.

Akira will fight back just as a green-haired man with sunglasses arrives on a motorbike. This is Akira's friend, Lawless, who joins our protagonist's fight against the masked gang members. A battle will begin. This is our first taste of Akira's fighting skills.

This fight shouldn't be too difficult, although it's a good excuse to get used to Akira and Lawless' move sets. The majority of Akira's attacks rely on his psychic abilities, while Lawless has a honed arsenal of physical attacks. Use Mother's Shame to damage the majority of the bikers (and potentially wipe a few out if you're lucky). Once the move has been executed, use both characters' various kicks and strikes to wipe the board clear.

After the fight is finished, Akira will thank Lawless, who will offer him a lift back to the orphanage. After Lawless climbs on his bike, read his mind and then Akira will climb onto the back of the vehicle. The scene will then cut to a gloriously over-the-top intro sequence before we arrive back at the orphanage.

Saving Tarokichi

After speaking to Lawless, head inside the orphanage. As you enter the main corridor, a cutscene will trigger, with Akira speaking to Taeko. Once the conversation has concluded, head to the right-hand side of the orphanage and look for a group of kids watching wrestling on the television.

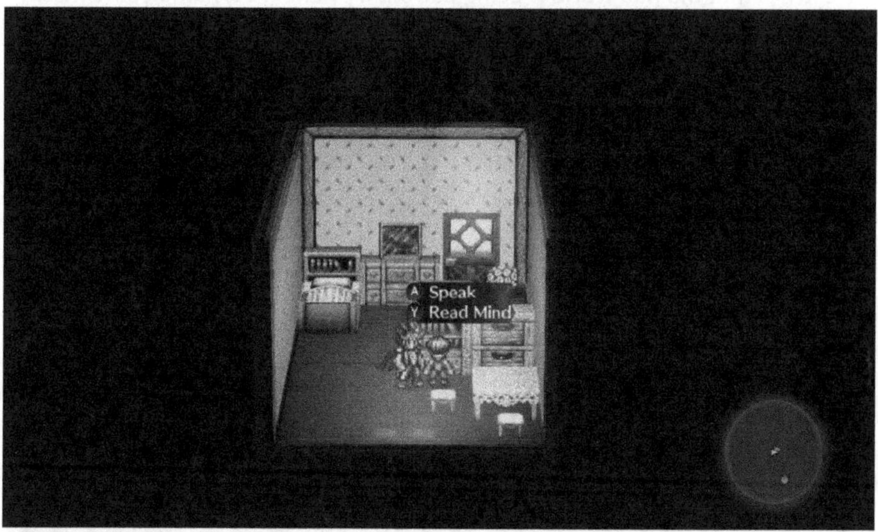

Speak to Watanabe (the kid sat on the far left). Akira will ask him to raid Taeko's room for something to patch him up. Watanabe will reluctantly agree, leaving to find the items. After Akira notes that Watanabe's been gone for a while, go look for him. You'll want to head back to the hallway and enter the first door south of Akira when heading down the west corridor. Inside, you'll find Watanabe. Speak to him.

Head back to the TV, stand directly in front of the screen and press A. A cutscene will trigger, with Yuki knocking into Akira. After it's done, Watanabe will return with the medical supplies, handing you a First Aid Kit. Take it and go to leave. Watanabe will then tell you that Kaori is upset about her pet turtle's illness. Head to the west side of the building and enter the last door at the end of the hallway. Inside you'll find Kaori crying about her turtle.

Akira will offer to speak to Doctor Tobei about the turtle, and so we have our next destination. Leave the orphanage and head out to the hub world. Let's quickly run through how this hub world works.

Hub World

The Near Future's hub world is a giant, traversable map of the city, with Akira able to walk to locations to advance the story, fight enemies or explore. To access a location, you simply walk into it and the area will load.

The catch is that the hub world is being patrolled by enemies; namely, the mask-wearing gang members we met earlier in the chapter. They'll chase you if you get too close and try to initiate a battle, so we can avoid or battle them if we wish.

For this current mission, we're looking to reach Dr Tobei's store: Timeless Wonders Antiques. It's a small wooden building located in the southwest corner of the map. As it's our objective, it's marked by a golden diamond on the mini-map. We can head there now or spend some time farming experience by defeating nearby enemies. It's up to you, although the latter will give you better standing against some of the challenges we'll face later on.

Once we do decide to visit Dr Tobei, head to his store. Once inside, proceed to the wooden door beside the sink at the back of the shop. Press Y to read Tobei's mind. After he finishes his "business", he'll come out to greet you. Speak to him until he runs down the stairs west of where the two of you are standing.

Follow him down the steps and stand in the centre of the big capsule beside him. It's hard to miss, but the machine has a red circular platform at its centre. After standing on the platform, the machine will blow up, much to the dismay of Tobei who will disappointedly send Akira home.

Transferring Tarokichi's Consciousness

Return to the orphanage and head to Kaori's room. Akira will tell his sister that Tobei is on the way to save her turtle. Seconds later, he'll enter the room. After examining the turtle, Tobei will claim the only way to save him is to turn the turtle into a robot (...I don't think this man has a PHD). He'll bring out a large robot and then hand Akira a plug, telling him to put it into a nearby socket.

The socket can be found just to the right of Kaori's door. Akira will insert the plug. This will electrify Tobei but successfully transfer Tarokichi's consciousness to the robotic body. This new robot-Tarokichi hybrid is known as Taroimo. Head over to Tobei once you regain control and read his mind. He'll see the success with the turtle bot and hatch a new plan, rushing off to his lab before we can learn what that grand idea is.

Now, read the robot's mind. It'll declare its undying gratitude to Kaori and then join the party, officially becoming a member of the crew. Seeing as we've just added Taroimo, let's quickly cover how he works. Unlike Akira, Taroimo doesn't level up. Instead, we'll have to find Robotic Enhancement modules that boost his stats. We'll accumulate these through battles and use them to enhance Taroimo by accessing them in the inventory. Don't use too many though. We can actually use them in the Final Chapter.

We can add attacks to Taroimo by finding Napalm and Fragmentation Grenades in enemy encounters. Later in the chapter, we'll discover a way to upgrade items, and we can upgrade these projectiles into new weapons for Taroimo.

Once you've become acquainted with Taroimo, exit Kaori's room and a cutscene will trigger. We'll see Taeko lecturing the children, instructing them to go to sleep. Another child will leave the room. Head through the door the child came out of and talk to Watanabe. He's the kid sleeping in the bed in the bottom left-hand corner of the room. He'll tell you to meet him in the bathroom later to discuss a plan.

Once you're done talking, leave this room and head towards the area with the TV. It's on the east side of the orphanage. Opposite the back of the TV, you'll see a door leading to the laundry room. Enter the room and speak with Taeko.

She'll leave the room shortly after. Now, search the laundry machine. You'll find a Matron's Crochet. After you've grabbed that, enter the door to the left of the laundry machine and grab the item by the bath to secure the Shampoo Hat.

With those items nabbed, return to the laundry room and then head through the door on your right. Walk towards the toilet and Akira will sit down and wait for Watanabe. When Watanabe arrives, he'll give you the Watanabe's Pocket Lint item. Akira will act disgusted at the item, telling Watanabe to try again. Once Watanabe leaves the room, leave the bathroom. After you're back in the Laundry Room, immediately return to the bathroom and sit on the toilet again.

Watanabe will return, this time giving you Taeko's Pouch. Once he's gone, leave the bathroom and return again. This time, Watanabe will give you Taeko's Picture. Rinse and repeat one more time and Taeko will walk in on Watanabe and Akira's secret meeting. She'll slap Akira, but Watanabe will still give us Taeko's Furious Fist. Once the scene's over, equip Taeko's Furious Fist in your weapon slot and equip Taroimo with Taeko's Pouch.

Now, let's leave the orphanage. Our objective now is to return to Dr Tobei and find out what his master plan was, but we can also spend some time accumulating experience and Robotic Enhancements. It's up to you, but it's well worth putting the time in to make sure this human-robot duo are as strong as possible.

Dr Tobei's Mech

When you're ready, head to Dr Tobei's store. Once inside, head down the stairs on the west side of the room and then use a second staircase at the back of this lower level. The next area will have a winding staircase leading down, so follow it all the way to the bottom floor and head through the door you find there.

Inside, we'll discover Dr Tobei looking at a giant mech. Approach the scientist and talk to him.

He'll inform us that powerful psychics used to pilot mechs. Isn't it handy that we know someone who seems to perfectly fit that very specific description??? Akira will offer his services and Tobei will ask whether he's up to the task. Agree and he'll ask you to meet him upstairs.

Head all the way back to the first floor of the shop and speak to Dr Tobei. He can be found just in front of the stairs reading some notes. He'll ask us to perform a series of bizarre tasks. Once we regain control, complete these steps in this order.

Touch the pink elephant statue in the top right-hand corner of the shop.

Read the note in front of Dr Tobei (you have to approach it on the side of the table opposite where he's standing)

Strike the xylophone on the table in the centre of the room

Touch the blue mask next to the red vase at the top of the stairs

Return to the mech on the bottom level of the store and offer it a prayer.

Return to the top floor and wash your hands in the sink at the back of the room.

Enter the washroom via the door next to the sink and sit on the toilet.

It's worth noting that every step bar the mech prayer takes place on the top floor. If you can't find something, it'll be in that room somewhere.

Once every step is complete and you're sat on the toilet, it'll begin to descend like an elevator, taking Akira, Taroimo and Tobei inside the head of the mech. Head over to the panel and press each switch.

There are two switches on the left and right sides of the panel and then a wheel you can operate in the middle. However, none of these will work for you just yet.

Optional: Item Upgrading

Speak to Tobei and he'll bring you back to the top floor of the antique shop. Once you arrive, he'll offer his services as an item upgrader, allowing us to make great items out of generic everyday junk. All you have to do is hand Tobei an item and he'll tinker with it. He isn't always successful, however, you won't lose the item by giving it to him, so just try again until he succeeds.

Some items actually have multiple outcomes, leaving it up to chance what you get. If you're looking to craft a lot of items very quickly, make sure to hold ZR to skip Tobei's dialogue. Here are some of the best items we can upgrade to get much better gear:

Item	Upgraded Item
Set of Sweats Taeko's Pouch	Punk Jacket Taeko's Picture
Punk Jacket Taeko's Picture	Biker's Belt
Biker's Belt	Jushin Wrestling Shirt
Baseball Glove	Bowling Ball
Bowling Ball	Taeko's Furious Fist
Napalm Grenade Fragmentation Grenade	100 Volt Laser Stun Gun Plasma Spark
100 Volt Laser Stun Gun Plasma Spark	Poison Spray

Poison Spray	A Jar of Kotobuki Lacquer Rock Launcher
A Jar of Kotobuki Lacquer Rock Launcher	Showa Goldfish Launcher Angel Bottle
Showa Goldfish Launcher Angel Bottle	Showa Chick Launcher

We can come back here whenever to add new items to our arsenal as we amass more loot, so feel free to stop back in anytime and gear up. For now though, let's leave the antique store. When we're back in the hub world, it's worth taking down some roaming enemies to amass new items we can upgrade.

Items like Napalm Bombs and Fragmentation Grenades can be upgraded into weapons for Taroimo, making him stronger, so it's worth scouting the area to make sure he's as powerful as possible. Once you've upgraded a few enhancements for Taroimo and Akira, equip them in the menu.

Optional: Selling Taiyaki

Speaking of items, we can actually head to the park we awoke in at the start of the chapter and sell taiyaki for Lawless. In return, he'll offer us an endless supply of healing items.

Upgrade these at the antique store, and we'll net some of the best healing items in the game. If you're interested, head to the Taiyaki Stand. It's in the centre of the park.

Stand behind it, speak to Lawless and then examine the grill to begin the activity. The basic gist here is to serve each customer that comes to the stand, adjusting the price based on who they are. Let's run through each customer and what price you should set.

If you get a young boy, charge him 100 yen. You'll get a Taiyaki in return.

If you get an old lady, charge her 100 yen. You'll get a Taiyaki in return.

If you get a businessman, charge him 1000 yen. You'll get a Guts and Glory Special in return.

If you get a woman, charge her 300 yen. You'll get a Banana Crepe in return.

You can keep doing this infinitely, which means unlimited healing items and much easier fights. Come here if you ever need to stock up. You can upgrade all healing items with Tobei, so head to his shop if you want the best items available.

Orphanage Kidnapping

When you're ready, head back to the orphanage. Once you arrive, proceed inside and walk towards the hallway. You'll hear a scream from outside. Leave through the front door and you'll see Kazu has been taken hostage by the Crusaders.

Walk towards Taeko and read her mind. Once you've seen the thought, Akira will tell Taeko to move as he and Taroimo take on the kidnappers. Once the battle begins, step between all three opponents and hit Behind You to end the battle before it's even begun.

The remaining two Crusaders will grab Kazu and flee on motorcycles just as Lawless arrives. He gives chase, as Akira and Taroimo steal a bike and race after him. Following a short cinematic chase sequence, we'll arrive at the City Docks.

Head to the southeast corner of the area and you'll hear Kazu shouting from behind you. Follow his voice north and we'll hear him scream again, this time being taken around the corner from Akira and Taroimo. Round the corner and head south. You'll hear Kazu again, with his kidnappers taking him west. Follow his scream. You'll hear another scream. Push west again until you reach the edge of the area, and then go north.

The scream this time with lead you south. Head to the very bottom of the screen until you trigger another scream, then head east. Run until you're next to Kazu, then follow his kidnapper south and out the area.

In the next section of the docks, you'll see Lawless cornering the four kidnappers. Walk over to him and you'll trigger a dialogue exchange. After some taunts, we'll have to fight the four kidnappers. The technique remains the same as usual. Use Behind You to hit the top three enemies, then use Lawless and Taroimo's melee moves to finish the pack off and deal with the final straggler.

Once the fight's finished, read the mind of the Crusader Lawless spoke to. He'll reveal that the reason they kidnapped Kazu was to find test subjects for a laboratory known as Tsukuba Lab. Tell Lawless about it. He'll be surprised. When he refuses to speak more on it, read his mind. You'll discover he intends to go to the lab alone. He'll then leave.

Head to the Orphanage and go to Kaori's room. Read her mind and she'll reveal that Lawless forced her not to reveal where he's going. Luckily, we already know that he's headed to the lab.

Tsukuba Lab

With this information, we have our heading. However, before we go, let's do a little bit of levelling and item gathering. We'll want to aim to get to around level 10 before we venture to the lab, so patrol the streets, fight some enemies and level up. If you've found any useful items, exchange them to Taeko for upgraded variations. We're specifically looking for Napalm Grenades, as we can kit these out into brand new weapons for Taroimo.

If you can get roughly 5 Napalm Grenades, we can get a good selection of weapons for Taroimo from Tobei, including the 100 Volt Laser, Plasma Spark, Kotobuki Lacquer, Showa Goldfish Launcher and Stun Gun. It's also worth finding some Robotic Enhancement modules and using them to buff up Taroimo. Head to Dr Tobei and refine everything (including all your healing items).

When you are ready, head across the bridge on the east side of the city. You'll find the lab on the other side. Head up to the two guards at the front gate. They'll ask whether you have an appointment. Pick "Appointment?" to get inside, causing Akira to start a fight with the two bodyguards.

Defeating these two is simple. Use a large AOE attack (Six Feet Under is the best shout if you have it, as the guards are resistant to Spirit attacks, making Behind You and Mother's Shame less effective). Avoid their attacks and execute a second AOE attack to finish the fight. Both enemies might drop an accessory known as a Poop Patrol Badge. If you get these, equip them on Akira. They'll boost his speed.

Once they're down, push ahead and take on the two guards watching the main door to the lab. Defeat them and enter the lab. Inside, you'll find yourself in a lobby. Take out both guards in this room for experience. They'll each join the battle with dogs, but you only have to kill the security guards to win the fight. Once they're both down, head through the doors on the right-hand side of the room.

You'll access a corridor with two doors south of you and an escalator on the east side of the area. Defeat the guard patrolling the corridor and enter one of the south doors. You'll wind up in an office. Loot the two lockers next to the door on the left-hand side. You'll find a Fragmentation Grenade and a Throwing Knife. Leave the office and head up the escalators on the east side of the room.

Once you reach the Second Floor, take the guard out and proceed through the door south of you. Follow the tunnel south, enter the next room and battle the two guards inside. When they're down, proceed down the escalator to your left. You'll arrive in a room with a single guarded door. Take down the guard and enter the door. You'll find a group of Crusaders looking for a fight.

You'll automatically enter a battle. There will be four Crusaders here and two robots, but we only need to take down the Crusaders. The numbers here can be overwhelming, however, if you hit Sleep in Heaven, you should put most of the enemy units to sleep. Considering the Crusaders we're battling our resistant to a lot of moves, our best bet is to use melee to wipe them out.

Have Taroimo take the units on the left and Akira fight the enemies above. Any melee hits should finish the Crusaders in one blow. Taroimo's Goldfish Shot is also very useful (if you have it), making short work of the Crusaders from range. Once the fight's over, Lawless will enter the room. After a short conversation, he'll officially join the party. Use the door he entered through and follow the path ahead. There will be five guards in green suits blocking your route. Battle them. Each guard encounter will be one of two battles:

The more common type sees you fight a guard and an army of RC cars. If you get this fight, you only have to take down the guard. Use Mother's Shame as Akira to clear a path through the line of RC cars and then use Lawless's Fists of Rage ability to kill the guard instantly.

The second battle type sees you take on just the guard. However, he's resistant to punch attacks and has a lot more health. In this case, use Akira's Feel the Heat ability and Taroimo's 100 Volt Laser to exploit his fire vulnerability and finish him fast. Once all the guards are finished, we'll find ourselves standing in front of three doors.

If you want more experience, head through the door on the right. Read the mind of the employee inside this room and you'll trigger an alarm, summoning a horde of guards. They're resistant to Spirit attacks, but weak to punch attacks, so use Lawless to carve through them with Fists of Rage.

Leave the room after you win the battle and enter the door on the left. Here, we'll find some secret labs that expose a little bit more about our enemy's objective.

Read the minds of the employees inside to get some interesting lore tidbits, then enter the room on the left-hand side. You'll find yourself in a lab filled with yellow tanks.

Find the scientist in the southwest corner and read his mind. He'll reveal a secret code: F-4-9-F. Now, head back to the corridor and examine the central door. Input the code we just found. It'll unlock the door.

Inside, we'll find three figures: General Yamazaki, a decaying scientist called Doctor Livingstill and a mysterious priest named Unryu. Listen to the trio share their evil plan and then they'll summon a mech to fight us.

Combat Unit W1 Boss Fight

So, there are two ways to beat this hunk of metal. We can cheese the robot or beat him legitimately. It's really up to you. First, let's run through the normal strategy:

Combat Unit W1's biggest strength is his health pool and resistance to some of Akira's best attacks. There's no point using Spirit or Demonic attacks against this lump of metal, as he'll resist. Over than that, it's fair game. Move Akira and Lawless in close to W1 and use Taroimo as ranged backup, staying just far back enough that he can land Goldfish Shot and 100 Volt Laser.

Hit him with any attacks that deal medium or high damage. For Akira, that means Cold Day in Hell, Holy Smackdown (if you have it) or Feel the Heat, while Lawless can use Fists of Rage, Badass Kicks or Gut Punch. W1 will execute melee attacks from here, but it's nothing you can't take. Heal when anyone's hurting and you shouldn't have much trouble.

His most brutal attack is his Missile attack he can hit at random near anywhere on the battlefield. However, if you keep Lawless below him, Akira to the right of him and Taroimo diagonal of him, he'll only be able to hit one of the three of you, allowing you to heal the fallen party member and keep the beatdown going. Continue hitting him with big attacks and he should go down in no time.

Now, if you aren't feeling a long fight with this metal foe, let's go through the much easier strat. All you have to do is get Akira to run behind the robot and use Elbow Strike on its back.

The robot will use Vaporise as a counter, exploding in the process and dying instantly. Essentially, it ends the fight before it's even started. It's really up to you which strategy you use.

Regardless of how we take him, the following cutscene will see us learn a tragic fact about W1 before he detonates. The group will then flee and we'll return to the Orphanage.

Point of No Return Warning

After the cutscene in the Orphanage, it's our official point of no return warning. We still have a few story beats to hit before the finale, but this is our last time to refine items and farm experience. The Near Future chapter is also unique in that it directly affects one character's potential in the Final Chapter.

For one, it's wise to unequip all of the additional weapons you've equipped on to Taroimo. We'll want these for the Final Chapter, as Cube can equip them. Don't worry. Taroimo doesn't have any more heavy lifting to do in this chapter, so he won't need them. It's also smart to farm Robotic Enhancements but don't spend them on Taroimo. Instead, keep them. We can use them on Cube later but they're much harder to find during the finale.

Spend some time refining items you found during your time in the lab. Fragmentation Grenades work similarly to Napalm Grenades and can be used to craft weapons we can later graft onto Cube.

Piloting the Steel Mech

When you're ready, head to Timeless Wonders Antiques and read Doctor Tobei's mind. He'll reveal that Lawless is drowning his sorrows in a nearby bar. You can find the establishment just north of the Orphanage. It's hard to miss as it has a neon sign above it reading "bar". Enter the building and head up the stairs.

You'll find Lawless on the left-hand side of the room at the top of the stairs. Read his mind. Once you have, leave the bar and you'll see a group of Crusaders have burnt down the Orphanage. Head over to the Orphanage and speak to the Matron. She'll tell you Kaori and Taeko are still inside.

After the kids have fled the scene, enter the Orphanage and run towards Kaori's room. You'll encounter Taeko on the way. Speak to her and then continue into the orphans' bedroom. It's the door to the right of where we found Taeko. Kaori is on the floor in the centre of the room. Read her mind and she'll get to her feet.

The scene will then cut to Lawless convincing Tobei to let him try to pilot the Steel Titan one last time. After consuming a pile of mantango, he'll manage to pilot the mech, using it to save Akira, Kaori and Taroimo from the orphanage. Once the scene's over and we regain control, we'll be inside the mech. Read Lawless' mind to discover a whole heap of backstory and a major reveal.

After it's done, Akira will command everyone to leave, using his psychic powers to pilot the Steel Titan. Enjoy Akira going super saiyan and we'll transition into the final stage of this chapter.

Reaching The Great Inko

From now on, we'll control the mech. We'll need to pilot it to the temple on the north side of the map. Enemies will litter the streets, although we'll be significantly stronger than every unit we encounter, so don't worry about them. Make a beeline straight through the centre of the city.

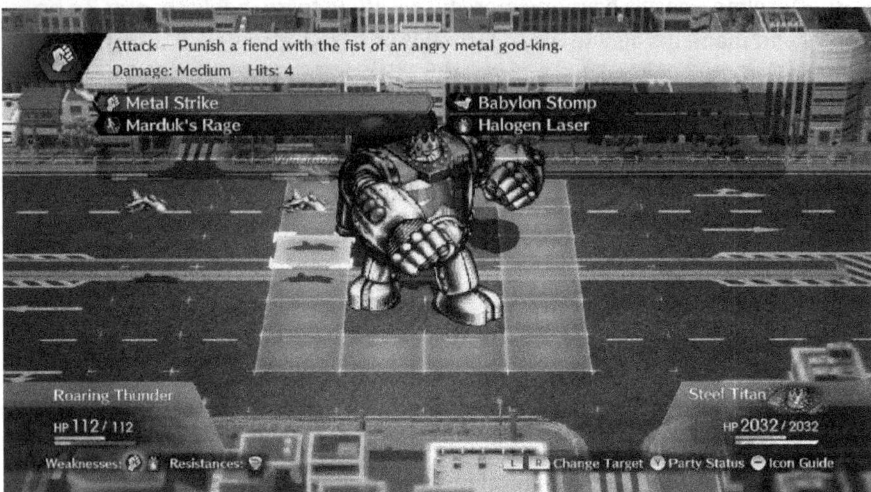

Use the coming fights to learn how the Steel Titan works in battle. You won't get EXP from the fights (the Steel Titan can't level up), but it's worth getting used to how he operates.

The Halogen Laser is an incredibly strong AOE that will fry anything even remotely close to you. Metal Strike is a melee strike that hits multiple times. Marduk's Revenge is a missile strike that barrages enemies and Babylon Stomp is a devastating jump attack that hits diagonally.

The only enemy here that will put up any fight is the Vengeful Dragon (the flying ship soaring around the streets). There's no reward for taking it down, but it's definitely an eyesore, so bring it to the ground if you'd like. Hit it with Metal Strike to exploit its weakness and end it quickly. When you're ready, head to the temple. You'll have to fight a second Vengeful Dragon before we can enter.

The Great Inko Boss Fight

When you arrive at the shrine, Livingstill, Unryu and Yamazaki will taunt you before summoning Odeo. The giant gold statue behind them will then come to life, initiating one final fight. Odeo's form (aka The Great Inko) will appear like a giant golden bird. Although it seems intimidating, this more violent incarnation of Big Bird is a bit of a pushover.

The vast majority of the fight will just be you and The Great Inko exchanging blows. He'll hit you with various forms of close quarters magic and will frequently bind you, preventing you from moving and using certain abilities. However, the strategy here is to just match his offence.

Marduk's Rage isn't much help due to The Great Inko's resistance to Projectile Attacks. However, Babylon Stomp, Halogen Laser and Metal Strike will all hit him hard. In particular, Babylon Stomp is your friend here. It will do a ton of damage to the Inko if you keep repeating it each turn. Keep laying in the damage and the Inko will inevitably fall.

Once the fight's done, we'll see one final cutscene showing the fates of Livingstill, Unryu, Yamazaki and Akira. Once the scene concludes, watch the credits and then the chapter will be complete. Congrats, it's time to pick your next character.

The Distant Future

Attempting to find his place on a spaceship transporting an extraterrestrial monstrosity and a mysterious saboteur that's got it out for the crew, Cube's Distant Future chapter is essentially a whodunnit visual novel set in deep space. It's easily Live A Live's most story-heavy chapter and comes complete with plenty of fun homages to classic sci-fi cinema.

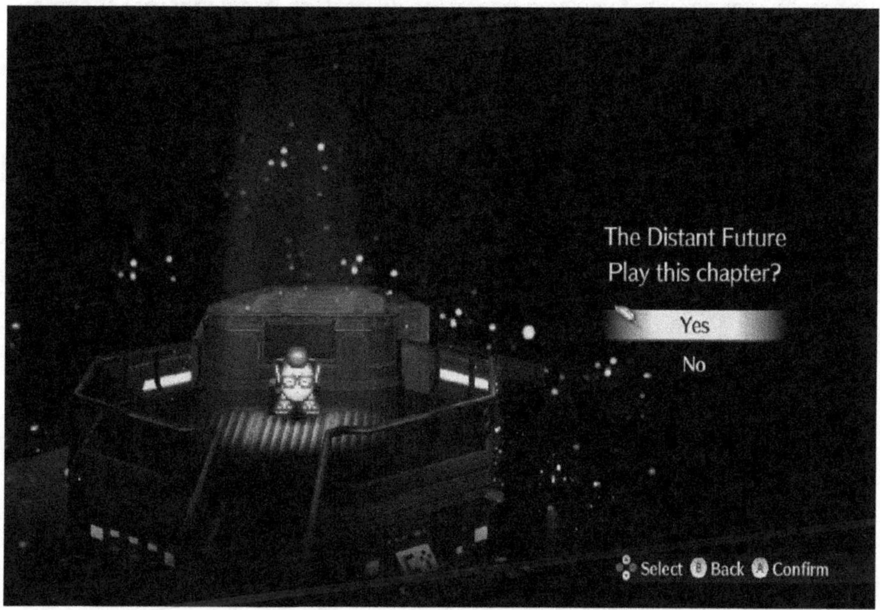

For those stuck trying to figure out where to go, who to talk to and how to advance the plot, the walkthrough below will give you all the pointers to help you finish Cube's mission and discover what's going on aboard the Cogito Ergo Sum.

You can skip between each section of the walkthrough by using the links below:

The Distant Future

This chapter is arguably the strangest of the lot. For one, there's no combat. Instead, this section largely focuses on story, dialogue and figuring out an eerie mystery. By and large, the gameplay mostly focuses on triggering events by visiting the right areas and speaking to the right people in the correct order.

It's easy to wonder what you're supposed to do next, so if in doubt, use the mini-map to figure out which character or event will trigger the next part of the story. Whichever character or location triggers the next story event will be marked by a gold diamond icon (as pictured above).

www.ingramcontent.com/pod-product-compliance
Lightning Source LLC
LaVergne TN
LVHW050559160826
845677LV00011B/2381

* 9 7 9 8 8 4 6 9 6 4 4 2 6 *